Mark Zuckerberg
In His Own Words

Mark Zuckerberg
In His Own Words

EDITED BY
George Beahm

AN AGATE IMPRINT

CHICAGO

Mark Zuckerberg: In His Own Words is in no way authorized, prepared, approved, or endorsed by Mark Zuckerberg and is not affiliated with or endorsed by any of his past or present organizations.

The first edition of this book was published in 2012 under the title *The Boy Billionaire*. This edition has been updated and expanded.

Mark Zuckerberg: In His Own Words
ISBN-13: 978-1-57284-262-5
ISBN-10: 1-57284-262-8

Printed in the United States of America

The Library of Congress has cataloged a previous edition of this book as follows:

The boy billionaire : Mark Zuckerberg in his own words / edited by George Beahm.
    pages cm
 Includes bibliographical references and index.
 Summary: "A collection of direct quotes from Mark Zuckerberg on topics related to business, technology, social media, and life collected from his own speeches, interviews, and writings"--Provided by publisher.
 ISBN 978-1-932841-76-3 (pbk.) -- ISBN 1-932841-76-8 (pbk.)
1. Zuckerberg, Mark, 1984- 2. Zuckerberg, Mark, 1984---Quotations. 3. Businesspeople--Quotations. 4. Social media--Quotations, maxims, etc. I. Zuckerberg, Mark, 1984- II. Beahm, George W.
 HM479.Z83B69 2012
 006.7092--dc23

10 9 8 7 6 5 4 3 2 1   18 19 20 21 22

B2 Books is an imprint of Agate Publishing. Agate books are available in bulk at discount prices. For more information, go to agatepublishing.com.

For Anne, Rachel, Hannah, and Sarah

Facebook was not originally created to be a company. It was built to accomplish a social mission—to make the world more open and connected. . . . We don't build services to make money; we make money to build better services.

—MARK ZUCKERBERG

Contents

Introduction: Facebook: Connecting the World......................1

Part I: Personal Life

On the Mark...16

Personal Challenges.....................................21

Parenting...27

Part II: Facebook Arrives

Starting Out..32

Facebook...51

Process..79

Part III: A Legacy in the Making

Mission...96

Values...113

Accountability..141

Vision..158

Philanthropy..180

Milestones..199

Introduction

Facebook: Connecting the World

THERE'S NEVER BEEN ANYTHING LIKE FACEBOOK. As of this writing, two billion people spend about an hour a day on the platform or its other services. Facebook is a community, a news source, a communal record of the world's celebrations, fears, frustrations, and controversies. The platform shows us what it thinks is important to us; it has a distinct and perhaps unprecedented role in deciding what we read and watch (and, some might say, think). And, because we give it so much of our own information—who we voted for, what our friends are like, where we live, where we went to school, where we work—it knows us in a way our own Facebook friends might not.

More and more, Facebook is a tool that its creators don't understand and can't always control. Since the 2016 US presidential election, when the Russian government planted ads and fake news stories on Facebook in an effort to influence the election's outcome, it's been clear that Facebook does not—or cannot—always follow its original stated mission of making the world "more open and connected." Mark Zuckerberg himself announced a new mission for Facebook in response to the divided atmosphere on the social media network during the elections: he now wants Facebook to "give people the power to build community and bring the world closer together."

Zuckerberg, the cofounder and CEO of Facebook, couldn't have predicted what Facebook would become when he first coded the website in his dorm room at Harvard in 2004. This book spans 16 years of Zuckerberg's public life, giving you a unique look into how this tech trailblazer's thoughts, opinions, and mindset have evolved over the years, much like the Facebook platform itself. Throughout the book, you'll see quotes from the era of Zuckerberg's meteoric rise to the top, from the times of Facebook's unprecedented success and innovation, and from periods of uncertainty and struggle, including new controversies such as Russian interference, mounting violence on the Facebook Live platform, and the leak of 50 million users' private data to Cambridge Analytica, a firm hired by the Donald Trump campaign that may have had a role in influencing the outcome of the election.

As Facebook has grown, so has Zuckerberg: from a fraternity member coding in his dorm room, he has turned into a philanthropist, a father, and the CEO of the world's biggest social network. It is fascinating to see the creator of Facebook reckon with what he's made, a platform that is altogether new and that still could achieve what its creator wants: a closer world.

The Early Years

Early on, it was clear to everyone that Mark Elliot Zuckerberg was special. The only son of Edward and Karen Zuckerberg, who also have three daughters, Mark was born in White Plains, New York, on May 14, 1984. (Coincidentally, it's the same year Apple Computer released its revolutionary Mac computer.)

Mark, as his father noted in the 2010 *Time* article which named Mark the Person of the Year, had always been intellectually demanding, even as a child. As Dr. Zuckerberg explained, if his son asked a question and the answer was "yes," no further elaboration was required; but a "no" required an explanation that had to be vigorously defended. Mark's interrogative ways might have suggested that they had a budding lawyer on their hands. It was a logical assumption, but their son's interests lay elsewhere: specifically, in the binary world of computer science.

At an early age, Mark's penchant for computers was obvious: at age 12, using Atari BASIC, he wrote a software program for messaging that was used at home and also at his father's dental practice. Called "Zucknet," it was the first "Mark Zuckerberg production"—a tagline that would originally run across the bottom of the early iterations of Zuckerberg's social media platform.

When his parents noticed their son's consuming interest in computer science, they hired a tutor—a software developer named David Newman who quickly realized that Mark was not your typical student but in fact a prodigy. Supplementing these lessons, Mark Zuckerberg also took a class in BASIC programming at nearby Mercy College. (When Dr. Zuckerberg took his son to school, he was told by the instructor that his son couldn't accompany him to class. Dr. Zuckerberg explained that Mark was the student, and not himself.)

Mark then transferred from Ardsley High School to a prestigious prep school, Phillips Exeter Academy (Exeter, New Hampshire), principally because it had a more robust computer science curriculum.

Even in sports, Zuckerberg seems to favor brains over brawn. At Phillips Exeter he started fencing, a sport that requires intense focus, quick reflexes, and hand-eye coordination. He went on to become captain of the fencing team.

He also developed a software application called Synapse, similar to Pandora. It attracted interest from Microsoft and AOL, resulting in offers to buy. Turning them down, Zuckerberg subsequently gave away the software for free.

Harvard

Zuckerberg entered Harvard as a freshman in fall 2002.

At first glance, given his obvious talent for computer science, nearby MIT (Massachusetts Institute of Technology) would seem a more suitable fit for Zuckerberg. Harvard, however, offered a more rounded curriculum, and he also had an interest in psychology—not surprising, since his mother is a former psychiatrist.

By Zuckerberg's sophomore year, he had earned a reputation as a computer geek after posting Course-Match online, which allowed students to see who was taking what courses.

As for Zuckerberg's personal life, he began dating Priscilla Chan, whom he would later marry in 2012.

Though CourseMatch brought Zuckerberg to the attention of his peers, it was his next project that put him on the radar of the Harvard community at large. To help with student identification, Harvard posted online directories of photographs called "Facebooks," individual mug shots of the student body.

After hacking into the official Facebooks, Zuckerberg

built a program called "Facemash" that posted photos of female students side by side, requiring the user to judge who was "hotter."

Wildly popular among his peers, the website drew outrage and calls to bring down the site from many groups on campus who vociferously complained to the administration. The site was shut down after only four hours of operation. It earned the puckish Zuckerberg an administrative hearing, after which he had to see a counselor.

What most people didn't know was that Harvard's students had gotten off comparatively easy: his original idea had been to post their photos with farm animals to judge the more attractive of the two. Zuckerberg abandoned that idea quickly, though, and ratcheted down to the slightly less offensive website idea.

The short-lived site firmly cemented Zuckerberg's reputation as the go-to guy for computer coding. It was then that he drew the attention of three upperclassmen who were developing a dating website exclusively for the Harvard community called HarvardConnection. Divya Narendra and twins Cameron and Tyler Winklevoss were looking to recruit a computer geek to quickly write code for their fledgling website. Time, they realized, was of the essence; they wanted to capitalize on having first-mover advantage. After seeing what Zuckerberg had done with Facemash, they realized they had found their man—or so they thought.

Zuckerberg agreed to work on the project, but he quickly put it on the backburner in favor of his own projects. After repeated queries that inevitably met with frustration due to Zuckerberg's delaying tactics, the HarvardConnection team realized that his priorities weren't aligned with theirs. Zuckerberg had moved on to other interests and intentionally disconnected from HarvardConnection.

What displaced Zuckerberg's interest in Harvard-Connection was his own social networking site called Thefacebook. Ensconced in Suite H33 at the Kirkland House dormitory, Zuckerberg and three colleagues worked in secrecy on the project. On January 11, 2004, they registered a domain, thefacebook.com, via register .com. It would be exclusively open to Harvard students with an email suffix of harvard.edu.

On February 4, 2004, Thefacebook went live, and Mark Zuckerberg's world was forever changed.

Janus

There's a classic *New Yorker* cartoon depicting a dog in front of a computer who says to another dog, "On the Internet, nobody knows you're a dog." The internet allows users to cloak themselves in anonymity, potentially fostering irresponsible or antisocial behavior such as stalking; posting libelous comments; initiating flame wars; and posting gratuitous, ugly, or racist comments.

To Zuckerberg, the dishonesty inherent in online anonymity was a major impediment to building a trusted community of online users. Requiring users to provide their actual email addresses insured transparency and reassured users, especially women.

The two-faced Roman god Janus comes to mind. Janus, who could simultaneously look at the past and the future, is a fitting symbol for Zuckerberg, who looked at the history of social networking online and saw that it would have no future if the web community remained in the dark ages by staying anonymous.

Moreover, Zuckerberg must have found it difficult to serve two increasingly demanding taskmasters: an academic course load as an undergrad, and Thefacebook, which was fast becoming his principal interest.

Words of Wisdom

In a significant, life-changing moment, chronicled in Ben Mezrich's marvelously inventive look at Facebook, *The Accidental Billionaires*, Microsoft's Bill Gates spoke to a gathering of students on campus. "After hemming and hawing a bit, Gates told the audience that the great thing about Harvard was that you could always come back and finish," wrote Mezrich.

The idea must have made sense to Zuckerberg, who saw it as a fail-safe option for Facebook. If he left Harvard and made the fledgling website succeed, fine; but if he left and Facebook failed, he could always return to the crimson fold of Harvard, finish his education, and get a well-paying job.

In June 2004 Mark Zuckerberg pulled the trigger. He left school and moved to Silicon Valley to work exclusively on Facebook, which then had a solid base of over a million users: the sky was the limit in terms of its potential.

Facebook's early success drew a lot of attention—especially from the Winklevoss twins, who filed a lawsuit in 2004 claiming copyright infringement. They contended that Mark Zuckerberg had brazenly stolen the basic idea of Facebook from them, and they were out to collect payment for the injustice.

The bitterly contested lawsuit, *Facebook, Inc. v. ConnectU, Inc.*, was initially dismissed, but ConnectU refiled, and the suit was eventually settled. Facebook paid an estimated $65 million in cash and stock shares. It was only afterward that incendiary instant messages by Zuckerberg surfaced. As Tyler Winklevoss told CNN's Piers Morgan in a February 8, 2011, interview, "At the time we settled, we had nowhere near the evidence that actually exists today. So we knew something had been done wrong. But what Facebook did throughout the entire litigation was suppress and withhold all the smoking gun electronic communications of Mark Zuckerberg."

Actually, the "smoking gun" was more of a misfire, according to *New Yorker* writer Jose Antonio Vargas. In "The Face of Facebook: Mark Zuckerberg Opens Up" (September 20, 2010), Vargas wrote, "Although the IMs did not offer any evidence to support the claim of theft, according to sources who have seen many of the messages, the IMs portray Zuckerberg as backstabbing, conniving, and insensitive."

The legal proceedings proved to be a distraction for Facebook and Zuckerberg, who had always proclaimed his innocence. To his way of thinking, Facebook and HarvardConnection were both social networking sites, but had little else in common. Zuckerberg asserted that the execution of the idea, and not the idea itself, was the essential difference, and he argued that his was the more popular website because it was simply more useful and embraced a larger virtual community.

Master of His Domain

When California witnessed a gold rush in 1848, hundreds of thousands of people were driven to seek their fame and fortune. California's current gold rush is found not in creek beds and gold nuggets, but in common sand—specifically, in silicon. Silicon Valley is a technological and financial epicenter located south of San Francisco. Financial angels, also known as venture capitalists, keep Silicon Valley alive by funding the dot-com dreams of hopeful entrepreneurs.

In 2004 Mark Zuckerberg and his friends moved to Palo Alto and rented a ranch-style house that served as both their personal residence and the office of the fledgling website. (They would later move into a nearby office building.) It was a modest beginning for what would be one of the biggest dot-coms of all time.

A year later, "Facebook was still just another smart ambitious startup," wrote Tomio Geron in a 2012 piece for Forbes.com, "The Untold Story of Two Early Facebook Investors." Facebook, he noted, had only 10 employees at that time.

Thefacebook got its jump-start when Zuckerberg appeared on a panel to discuss entrepreneurialism and startups at Stanford University, along with venture capitalist and Paypal cofounder Peter Thiel, entrepreneur Sean Parker, and venture capitalist Venky Harinarayan of Cambrian Ventures.

It was Harinarayan who told *Forbes* magazine, "The thing that surprised me the most was there were over 700 people in the audience. I've never seen so many people in one place at Stanford. Folks there were so passionate about Facebook I was absolutely stunned. ... I remember talking to Accel [an investment firm] after. The key reason they invested was because they talked to Stanford students and found out that they use Facebook for two hours a day."

In May 2005 Harinarayan and his partner Anand Rajaraman invested in Facebook, shortened from "Thefacebook" on Sean Parker's recommendation. Going in with Accel, the investment was to the tune of $12.7 million—sweet music to Zuckerberg's ears. Now his company had sufficient operating capital to properly launch the company and position it for significant future growth. Up until then, Facebook's reach had been deliberately restricted to a handful of universities, but when it opened up to other colleges and high schools both in the United States and abroad, the company soon attracted 5.5 million users. It was December 2005, and Facebook's rapid growth captured the attention of larger companies looking to acquire potentially lucrative dot-coms.

For the next seven years, Facebook fended off suitors as it continued to increase its user base, expand its products and services, and build momentum for its eventual IPO.

During that time, Facebook needed money, and a lot of it, because of the increasing demand for computer servers and support infrastructure. Despite the pressures from third-party companies who wooed Zuckerberg, he remained steadfast. Facebook was not for sale because it was positioning itself for its eventual IPO.

Facebook's Changing Stock

According to *Forbes* (May 2012), Facebook's IPO, on May 18, 2012, was the third largest in history, eclipsed only by Visa and Enel (a power company). Early investors had a lot to smile about during Facebook's IPO, though their joy didn't last long because, by November 2012, Facebook's stock was worth half its original price—$19.50 per share, down from $38.20.

Zuckerberg didn't speak publicly about the IPO for months. "Painful," was eventually his first comment regarding the stock's drop, during a mid-August 2012 staff meeting. However, Zuckerberg remained focused on the long term, reassuring employees and investors that the company would be profitable once its newly developed mobile platform (and, more importantly, ads tailored for mobile) hit its stride. Now, about 85% of Facebook's revenue comes from mobile, and Facebook has proven that it has the staying power to weather the stock market.

Concerns about Facebook don't center on profitability anymore. Instead, controversies and some of the CEO's own decisions have, over the years, caused fluctuations in Facebook's value. Zuckerberg's plans to sell his stock to fund the Chan Zuckerberg Initative, and to create a new class of nonvoting stock, affected stock prices as shareholders feared they would lose influence over the company. Zuckerberg later dropped his plans to reclassify the stock, and share prices continued on their consistent upward trajectory.

More recently, stock prices have dropped because shareholders are afraid Facebook has lost its users' trust. Prices went down after news outlets started reporting on Russian interference, how fake news spread on the platform, and the Cambridge Analytica data breach. After news of the Cambridge Analytica leak got to investors in March, the stock price dropped by about

14 percent and experienced its biggest one-day drop since the IPO in 2012. Many analysts, however, predicted that the breach would not affect Facebook's value in the long term.

Facebook's Election

The November 2016 election of Donald Trump came as a surprise to many people, perhaps including Zuckerberg. But in the months following the election, his website seemed to have been more or less instrumental to Trump's rise. While Zuckerberg initially prevaricated, citing all the good Facebook had done in getting people to vote, he eventually admitted that Facebook may have a far-reaching problem. Facebook discovered evidence that fake news about Trump and Hillary Clinton had been planted on the site by Russian actors who, according to US intelligence officials, sought to influence the election in Trump's favor. Facebook later admitted that at least 126 million Facebook users had seen ads or fake news planted by Russian interference. In her memoir *What Happened*, Clinton herself laid some of the responsibility for Trump's win with Facebook, criticizing the service for allowing Russian bots to infiltrate it.

The social network used by more than 2 billion people had apparently gotten out of control—Zuckerberg and his key staff were asleep at the wheel. The CEO vowed to take action, announcing enhanced security measures, more transparent political ad funding, and close monitoring of Facebook during elections across the world to ensure it didn't happen again. Facebook, clearly, had missed its mark.

In March 2018, it was also revealed that Cambridge Analytica, an advertising firm that was hired to help Trump win the presidential election, had been able to access 50 million users' private information. While data security had always been a concern for users and for Facebook, this was perhaps the first time that a data breach of such magnitude occurred. While it wasn't clear how the data was used, Facebook, without its knowledge or control, may have played a role in helping Trump win the election.

It wasn't just Russian interference and data leaks Zuckerberg was worried about. He denounced the divisive spirit in the country that took root in the country before, during, and after the election and that found fertile ground on Facebook. Zuckerberg had always wanted to use Facebook to build community; instead, it was being used to foment disagreement. In response, Facebook changed its algorithms so users would be more likely to see posts from their friends instead of from news outlets (especially outlets that spread fake news). Zuckerberg traveled the country to talk to pastors in Texas, students in Chicago, and lumber workers in Maine, among many others, about their own communities. Indeed, such an outreach struck some as being so atypical of Zuckerberg that they felt it might have signaled that he was going to run for president himself, which he flatly denied. The "meet and greet" by Facebook's cofounder and CEO was in fact an attempt to build the kind of community Zuckerberg saw across the country on his own social media network.

"Our goal is to make a change in the world."

Zuckerberg's Facebook has come a long way from its humble origins as a social medium catering to Ivy League students. Since it went public in 2012, Facebook has mutated, evolving into a virtual electronic village worldwide, as prophesied by Marshall McLuhan, who said of TV, the "global village's" first iteration, that "There's an earthquake and no matter where we live, we all get the message. And today's teenager, the future villager, who feels especially at home with our new gadgets—the telephone, the television—will bring our tribe even closer together."

The second iteration of this social medium, the internet, allowed worldwide interaction in real time, becoming the ultimate realization of McLuhan's global village.

Unquestionably, it is Facebook's reach as a social medium with over 2 billion users worldwide that will fulfill Mark Zuckerberg's dream of bringing that world together or, if mishandled, has the potential of tearing it apart.

Only time will tell.

Part I

PERSONAL LIFE

On the Mark

A LOT OF boys when they're younger have, like, Ninja Turtles or some toys and they're all, like, fighting? I just wanted to make them connect and, like, form villages and be peaceful and communicate. I was like, "Why can't you guys just talk to each other and work out your problems?"

—*Esquire*, September 23, 2015

MY YOUNGER SISTER bet me that she was going to finish college before me, which probably should have been a bad sign. But my parents apparently bet my sister that I was never going to finish college, which is really not, like, a lot of faith from your parents.

—Sequoia High School, September 18, 2014

I THINK LOTS of people confuse happiness with fun. I don't believe it is possible to have fun every day. But I do believe it is possible to do something meaningful that helps people every day.

—*Esquire*, September 23, 2015

I JUST WANT to focus on what we're doing.
When I put ["Eliminating desire"] in my profile,
that's what I was focused on. I think it's probably
Buddhist? To me it's just—I don't know, I think
it would be very easy to get distracted and get
caught up in short-term things or material
things that don't matter. The phrase is actually,
"Eliminating desire for all that doesn't really
matter."

—*Time*, December 27, 2010/January 3, 2011

ALL OF MY friends who have younger siblings
who are going to college or high school—my
number one piece of advice is: You should learn
how to program.

—*Charlie Rose*, November 7, 2011

I MAKE THINGS.

—Google+ profile, *Time: Techland*, July 5, 2011

I have a way of making things more intense than they should be.

—Facebook Live video, June 14, 2016

I WEAR THE gray shirt either when I'm going
to work or during the weekday, and the idea is I
don't want to really have to spend that much time
thinking about what I'm wearing.

—Facebook Live video, October 9, 2016

IF YOU COUNT the time I'm in the office, it's
probably no more than 50–60 hours a week.
But if you count all the time I'm focused on our
mission, that's basically my whole life.

—Facebook comment, April 14, 2015

Personal

Challenges

EVERY YEAR, I try to take on a personal challenge, right. And the reason is, I think it's really important to push yourself to learn and improve, both personally and in work. And, you know, I think it would be easy, running Facebook, to spend all my time on Facebook.

—**University of Kansas, November 10, 2017**

LAST YEAR . . . my personal challenge was to learn Chinese. I blocked out an hour every day to study and it has been an amazing experience so far. I've always found learning new languages challenging, so I wanted to jump in and try to learn a hard one. It has been a very humbling experience. With language, there's no way to just "figure it out" like you can with other problems— you just need to practice and practice. The experience of learning Mandarin has also led me to travel to China, learn about its culture and history, and meet a lot of new interesting people.

—*Fortune*, **May 26, 2011**

[T]HE ONLY MEAT I'm eating is from animals I've killed myself. So far, this has been a good experience.... Every year I have a yearly personal challenge. It's a good way to explore different things I wouldn't normally do and challenge myself. Toward the end of last year I reflected a bunch on how thankful I was that we were building so many good things and things have gone well so far and I decided to make this year's challenge around being more thankful for what I have. I struggled for a while about how to implement this, but eventually decided that forcing myself to get personally involved and thank the animals whose lives I take in order to eat them was the best day-to-day way to remind myself to be thankful.

—comment on Zuckerberg's Facebook page,
Fortune, May 4, 2011

MY PERSONAL CHALLENGE this year was A Year of Books—to read a new book every other week.

Reading has given me more perspective on a number of topics—from science to religion, from poverty to prosperity, from health to energy to social justice, from political philosophy to foreign policy, and from history to futuristic fiction.

—Facebook post, December 27, 2015

MY PERSONAL CHALLENGE for 2016 was to build a simple AI to run my home—like Jarvis in *Iron Man*.

My goal was to learn about the state of artificial intelligence—where we're further along than people realize and where we're still a long ways off.

—Facebook post, December 19, 2016

My personal challenge for 2017 is to have visited and met people in every state in the US by the end of the year. I've spent significant time in many states already, so I'll need to travel to about 30 states this year to complete this challenge.

—**Facebook post, January 3, 2017**

This year, the big impulse [behind my challenge] was really that I just kind of felt like I wanted to be in better touch with what people were thinking about their lives and their work and their future. And it was a funny thing, running a company like this—I'm much more likely to travel to big cities in other countries and talk to people who are like me than I am to go talk to people who have very different lives in our own country.

—*Masters of Scale*, **May 25, 2017**

THE TONE OF the campaigns leading up to 2016 and the election, I think, was just really surprising in terms of how divisive it was, no matter which side you were on. And it just led me to want to get out of my bubble in San Francisco and try to understand more of what was going on around the country.

—**University of Kansas, November 10, 2017**

I THINK I started this year [of travel] as an engineer, and now I'm wrapping it up thinking of myself as more of a community builder, too.

—**University of Kansas, November 10, 2017**

IN TERMS OF doing work and in terms of learning and evolving as a person, you just grow more when you get more people's perspectives. ... I really try and live the mission of the company and ... keep everything else in my life extremely simple.

—*Charlie Rose*, **November 7, 2011**

Parenting

WE'VE BEEN TRYING to have a child for a couple of years and have had three miscarriages along the way.

You feel so hopeful when you learn you're going to have a child. You start imagining who they'll become and dreaming of hopes for their future. You start making plans, and then they're gone. It's a lonely experience. Most people don't discuss miscarriages because you worry your problems will distance you or reflect upon you— as if you're defective or did something to cause this. So you struggle on your own.

In today's open and connected world, discussing these issues doesn't distance us; it brings us together. It creates understanding and tolerance, and it gives us hope.

—Facebook post, July 31, 2015

I'VE DECIDED TO take 2 months of paternity leave when our daughter arrives.

Studies show that when working parents take time to be with their newborns, outcomes are better for the children and families. At Facebook we offer our US employees up to 4 months of paid maternity or paternity leave which they can take throughout the year.

—Facebook post, November 20, 2015

BEING A PARENT is very much about imparting values.

—University of Kansas, November 10, 2017

CHILDHOOD IS MAGICAL. You only get to be a child once, so don't spend it worrying too much about the future. You've got us for that, and we'll do everything we possibly can to make sure the world is a better place for you and all children in your generation.

—letter written to daughter August Zuckerberg,
August 2017

WHEN PRISCILLA AND I first found out she was pregnant again, our first hope was that the child would be healthy. My next hope was that it would be a girl. I cannot think of a greater gift than having a sister and I'm so happy Max and our new child will have each other.

—Facebook post, March 9, 2017

IT'S IMPORTANT TO me that when Max and August grow up that they feel like what their father built was good for the world.

—*New York Times*, January 11, 2018

SOME DAYS I wake up and I just want to be with my daughter and teach her about the world. Some nights I go to bed and I'm not sure I made the right choices that day. I can tell you, those doubts don't go away, no matter who you are. But every day you just get up and try to make the world a little better.

—Facebook Community Summit, June 22, 2017

Part II

FACEBOOK ARRIVES

Starting Out

WELL I DON'T know business stuff.... I'm content to make something cool.

—instant messages to a friend, *Business Insider*,
January 8, 2004

[9:48 P.M.] I'M a little intoxicated, not gonna lie. So what if it's not even 10 p.m. and it's a Tuesday night? What? The Kirkland [dormitory] facebook is open on my desktop and some of these people have pretty horrendous facebook pics. I almost want to put some of these faces next to pictures of farm animals and have people vote on which is more attractive. [11:09 p.m.] Yea, it's on. I'm not exactly sure how the farm animals are going to fit into this whole thing (you can't really ever be sure with farm animals), but I like the idea of comparing two people together. [12:58 a.m.] Let the hacking begin.

—posted after being dumped by his girlfriend,
Zuckerberg's blog posts, *Huffington Post*,
February 4–5, 2004

My GOAL IS not to have a job. Making cool things is just something I love doing, and not having someone tell me what to do or a timeframe in which to do it is the luxury I am looking for in my life.... I assume eventually I'll make something that is profitable.

—*Harvard Crimson*, June 10, 2004

NOVEMBER 30, 2003: I read over all the stuff you sent and it seems like it shouldn't take too long to implement, so we can talk about that after I get all the basic functionality up tomorrow night.

DECEMBER 1: I put together one of the two registration pages so I have everything working on my system now. I'll keep you posted as I patch stuff up and it starts to become completely functional.

DECEMBER 4: SORRY I was unreachable tonight. I just got about three of your missed calls. I was working on a problem set.

DECEMBER 10: THE week has been pretty busy
thus far, so I haven't gotten a chance to do much
work on the site or even think about it really, so
I think it's probably best to postpone meeting
until we have more to discuss. I'm also really busy
tomorrow so I don't think I'd be able to meet then
anyway.

ONE WEEK LATER: Sorry I have not been
reachable for the past few days. I've basically
been in the lab the whole time working on a cs
[computer science] problem set which I'm still
not finished with.

JANUARY 8, 2004: Sorry it's taken a while for me
to get back to you. I'm completely swamped with
work this week. I have three programming projects
and a final paper due by Monday, as well as a couple
of problem sets due Friday. I'll be available to
discuss the site again starting Tuesday.

I'm still a little skeptical that we have enough
functionality in the site to really draw the
attention and gain the critical mass necessary to
get a site like this to run.

—**emails sent to the HarvardConnection team,**
Business Insider

I DO STUFF like this all the time. The facebook literally took me a week to make.... Half the things I do I don't release. I spent five hours programming last night, and came up with something that was kind of cool, showed it to a bunch of my friends, and the rest of the campus will never know about it.... I just like making it and knowing that it works and having it be wildly successful is cool, I guess, but I mean, I dunno, that's not the goal.

—*Harvard Crimson,* June 10, 2004

WE HAD A very simple focus and idea: The goal wasn't to make a huge community excited; it was to make something where you could type in someone's name and find out a bunch of information about them.... We ran the site originally for $85 a month, renting computers for the first three months. I was in debt $160, you know.

—*Our Time,* 2005

WHEN I WAS getting started, with my roommates in college, you never think that you could build this company or anything like that, right? Because, I mean, we were college students, right? And we were just building stuff 'cause we thought it was cool. I do remember having these specific conversations with my friends where we thought, you know, someone is gonna build this. Someone is gonna build something that makes it so that people can stay connected with their friends and their family, but no way would we be the ones who were contributing to, kinda, leading the whole Internet in this direction.

—*60 Minutes*, December 1, 2010

You know, in college, I just built a whole lot
of different things. And that's just a passion of
mine. It's, kind of, building things very quickly.
... We [Zuckerberg and his early collaborators]
figured, "Okay, this is something that may could
grow to be a lot bigger." And that's ... when my
roommates joined me and we really started
growing it aggressively.

—*Business Insider*, October 14, 2010

I also hate the fact that I'm doing it for other
people haha. Like I hate working under other
people. I feel the right thing to do is finish the
facebook and wait until the last day before I'm
supposed to have their thing ready and then be
like "look yours isn't as good as this so if you want
to join mine you can ... otherwise I can help you
with yours later." Or do you think that's too dick?

—on HarvardConnection, instant message to Adam
D'Angelo via *Business Insider*, fall 2002

IN COLLEGE I was a psychology major at the same time as being a computer science major. I say that fairly frequently, and people can't understand it. It's like, obviously I'm a CS person! But I was always interested in how those two things combined. For me, computers were always just a way to build good stuff, not like an end in itself.

—*Time*, December 27, 2010/January 3, 2011

WHEN I WAS in college I did a lot of stupid things, and I don't want to make an excuse for that. Some of the things that people accuse me of are true, some of them aren't. There are pranks, IMs. I started building [Facebook] when I was around 19 years old, and along the way, a lot of stuff changed. We went from a building a service in a dorm room to running a service that 500 million people use.

—D8 Conference, 2010

THERE ARE A few other things that I built when I was at Harvard that were kind of smaller versions of Facebook. One such program was this program called CourseMatch. People could enter the different courses that they were taking, and see what other courses would be correlated with the courses they are taking. And over my time at Harvard I built programs like that. On a small scale.

—*Fast Company*, September 17, 2009

I MAINTAIN THAT he fucked himself. . . . He was supposed to set up the company, get funding, and make a business model. He failed at all three. . . . Now that I'm not going back to Harvard I don't need to worry about getting beaten by Brazilian thugs. . . . Eduardo is refusing to co-operate at all. . . . We basically now need to sign over our intellectual property to a new company and just take the lawsuit. . . . I'm just going to cut him out and then settle with him. And he'll get something I'm sure, but he deserves something. . . . He has to sign stuff for investments and he's lagging and I can't take the lag.

—emails to Dustin Moskovitz and a third party,
Business Insider, 2004

As FAR AS Eduardo goes, I think it's safe to ask him to ask his permission to make grants. Especially if we do it in conjunction with raising money. It's probably even OK to say how many shares we're adding to the pool. It's probably less OK to tell him who's getting the shares, just because he might have [an] adverse reaction initially. But I think we may even be able to make him understand that. Is there a way to do this without making it painfully aware to him that he's being diluted to 10%?

—email to a lawyer, *Business Insider*, 2005

INSTEAD, FROM THESE conversations, it became apparent that [they] were not as clued-in and business-savvy as they had led me to believe. It almost seemed like my most socially inept friends at the school had a better idea of what would attract people to a website than these guys. ... After that meeting I began making thefacebook, and I did not hear from them until about one week ago when I received their demand letters, threatening to bring me before the [Harvard] ad board on ethical grounds.

As a bit of background, I try not to get involved with other students' ventures since they are generally too time-consuming and don't provide me with enough room to be creative and do my own thing.

Frankly, I'm kind of appalled that they're threatening me after the work I've done for them free of charge, but after dealing with a bunch of other groups with deep pockets and good legal connections including companies like Microsoft, I can't say I'm surprised. I try to shrug it off as a minor annoyance that whenever I do something successful, every capitalist out there wants a piece of the action.

—on the HarvardConnection team, email to
Harvard dean John Walsh, February 17, 2004

YOU KNOW, IT'S hard for me to fully wrap my head around where they're coming from on this. You know, early on, they had an idea that was completely separate from Facebook. And that, I mean, it was a dating site for Harvard. And I agreed to help them out with it, to help them. Right, I mean, it wasn't a job, they weren't paying me, I wasn't hired by them or anything like that. And then, the idea that I would then go work on something completely different, like Facebook, and that they would be upset about this all these years later is kinda mindboggling for me. Now, I mean, this is another thing that I think the movie [*The Social Network*] really missed is, I mean, they make it seem like this whole lawsuit is such a huge part of Facebook's history. I've probably spent less than two weeks of my time worried about this lawsuit at all, right? . . . I mean, after all this time, I feel bad that they still feel bad about it.

—on the Winklevoss brothers' out-of-court settlement
worth a reported $65 million and their further claim
that they were ripped off, *60 Minutes*, December 1, 2010

There's this culture in the [Silicon] Valley of starting a company before they know what they want to do. You decided you want to start a company, but you don't know what you are passionate about yet. ... You need to do stuff you are passionate about. The companies that work are the ones that people really care about and have a vision for the world, so do something you like.

—Startup School, October 29, 2011

THE POINT THAT I was trying to make wasn't
that I couldn't have necessarily started Facebook
in Boston or stayed here; it was that I think that
there is more than one place where people can
build companies. There's a feeling in Silicon
Valley that you have to be there, because that's
where all the engineers are. I just don't know if
that's true. I think a lot of good companies get
started all over the place. And often, I think a
lot of people move out to Silicon Valley because
that's where they have to be, but there's so many
smart people out here at MIT, Harvard, and other
universities that you can start a company here,
you can start a company in New York, you can
start it in any country you want. That's basically
the point I was trying to make.

—**MIT, November 8, 2011**

THERE ARE ASPECTS of the culture out here [in Silicon Valley] where I think it still is a little bit short-term focused in a way that bothers me. … I think there's this culture out here where people don't commit to doing things. And there's nothing wrong with experimentations here—you need to do that before you dive in and decide that you're going to do something, but I feel like a lot of the companies that have built outside of Silicon Valley seem to be on a longer-term cadence than the ones in Silicon Valley for whatever reason.

—Startup School, October 29, 2011

WE WEREN'T EVEN set up as a company at first. I started it with different friends at Harvard who were really smart, and they didn't have the same levels of commitment. I moved to Silicon Valley, lots of folks didn't want to move out. A lot of the early founder group was fractured. I didn't want to be involved with setting up the business at all. We had this guy Eduardo. Instead of setting up a standard company, we set up as a Florida LLC. I don't know all the things wrong with that, but lawyers out here said that was number one to unwind.

—on the "dumb things" he did when starting Facebook, Startup School, October 29, 2011

INSTEAD OF LAUNCHING schools that would
be most receptive, we did least receptive. We
launched at Stanford, Columbia, Yale, where
each of them had their own community already.
When we launched Facebook at those schools
and it took off, we realized it could be worth
putting our time into it. My friends are people
who like building cool stuff. We always have
this joke about people who want to just start
companies without making something valuable.
There's a lot of that in Silicon Valley. We wanted
to be valuable.

—Startup School, October 29, 2011

I THINK IT took a year for us to get 1 million users,
and we thought that that was incredibly fast. And
I think it is, but it wasn't as quick as a lot of things
grow today. And I think actually having that time
to bake it was really valuable for us.

—Startup School, October 20, 2012

WHEN WE GOT started, everyone compared us to MySpace. The big difference that we saw between ourselves and MySpace was that people used MySpace because it was cool and because it was fun. People ask us this question all the time: What's going to happen when Facebook is no longer cool? My answer to that question is that our goal is never to build something cool; it's to build something *useful*. Something that's cool is not going to be around for a long time. Something that's useful is around for a very long time potentially, if it continues to be useful. So when I say "utility," that's what I mean: We're trying to provide people with utility, not have something that's fun.

—Computer History Museum, July 21, 2010

Facebook

It isn't a core human need to use Facebook. It's a core human need to stay connected with the people you care about. The need to open up and connect is such a deep part of what makes us human. Being in a position where we are the company—or one of the companies— that can play a role in delivering that service is just ... an honor.

—*Bloomberg Businessweek,* October 4, 2012

I THINK THE biggest difference between Facebook and other companies is how focused we are on our mission. . . . Different companies care about different things. There are companies that care about, just really care about having the biggest market cap. Or there are companies that are really into process or the way they do things. Hewlett Packard, right? The thing that you always hear about them is "the HP Way." Google, I think, is very tied to their culture—they really love that. For us, it is the mission: building a company that makes the world more open and connected. The articulation of that has, I think, changed over time. But that's really been, like, the belief the whole time.

—*Huffington Post*, May 14, 2012

As a COMPANY we're very focused on what we're building and not as focused on the exit. We just believe that we're adding a certain amount of value to people's lives if we build a very good product. That's the reason why more than half of our users use the product every day—it's a more efficient way for them to communicate with their friends and get information about the people around them than anything else they can do. We're not really looking to sell the company. We're not looking to IPO anytime soon. It's just not the core focus of the company.

—*Time,* July 17, 2007

IF OUR MISSION is to make the world more open and connected, I certainly think that starts with us ourselves. We have this very open culture at the company. Every Friday afternoon, I get up and do a Q&A where anyone in the company can get up and ask me anything they want. One of the things I'm taking away from this is that if we want to lead the world and be the best service for this kind of sharing, that we should really probably be doing a lot more of it ourselves. I wouldn't characterize it as being a pitchman; I couldn't do that if I wanted to. But more open communication is good.

—*Time*, May 27, 2010

WELL, FACEBOOK IS all about focus and not a lot of bureaucracy, so when we first started having our board meetings a few years back what I'd do is just start writing down a summary of what was going on with the business on a yellow piece of paper and give it to the board, and we used to have these really focused, great discussions of what was going on. Since then the board meetings have gotten a bit more structured: there's a bit more information handed out. But at the end of all the meetings our directors just say, "You know, I still love that single piece of paper with a summary of what's going on."

—*Fast Company*: 30 Second MBA, March 2, 2012

I THINK THAT people just have this core desire to express who they are. And I think that's always existed.

—*Charlie Rose*, November 7, 2011

ONE DEFINITION OF technology that I think is interesting is it extends some natural human capacity.... A social network, I think, extends people's very real social capacity.

—Startup School, October 20, 2012

- YOU HAVE CONTROL over how your information is shared.
- We do not share your personal information with people or services you don't want.
- We do not give advertisers access to your personal information.
- We do not and never will sell any of your information to anyone.
- We will always keep Facebook a free service for everyone.

—core principles of Facebook, *Washington Post*, May 24, 2010

IT'S REALLY THE people themselves who have gotten us to this state. I mean, we've built a lot of products that we think are good and will help people share photos and share videos and write messages to each other. But it's really all about how people are spreading Facebook around the world in all these different countries. And that's what's so amazing about the scale that it's at today.

—*ABC World News*, July 21, 2010

WE HAVE THIS stat that we throw out all the time here: There is on the order of 1,000 engineers and now on the order of a billion users, so each engineer is responsible for a million users. You just don't get that anywhere else.

—*Bloomberg Businessweek*, October 4, 2012

ON AVERAGE, PEOPLE on the Facebook in the
US spend around 40 minutes each day using
our service, including about one in five minutes
on mobile. This is more than any other app by
[far], but overall people in the US spend about
nine hours per day engaging with digital media
on TVs, phones and computers. So there is a
big opportunity to improve the way that people
connect and share.

—quarterly earnings call, July 23, 2014

THAT'S JUST, LIKE, not something we're really
interested in. I mean, yeah, we can make a bunch
of money—that's not the goal ... I mean, like,
anyone from Harvard can get a job and make a
bunch of money. Not everyone at Harvard can
have a social network. I value that more as a
resource more than, like, any money.

—*Harvard Crimson*, June 10, 2004

Helping people connect is more important than maximizing the time they spend on Facebook.

—Facebook post, January 31, 2018

[ACQUIRING INSTAGRAM] IS an important milestone for Facebook because it's the first time we've ever acquired a product and company with so many users. We don't plan on doing many more of these, if any at all. But providing the best photo sharing experience is one reason why so many people love Facebook and we knew it would be worth bringing these two companies together.

—Facebook press release, April 9, 2012

FACEBOOK USED TO be this single blue app that did a lot of different things. Now, Facebook is a family of apps. More than 1.4 billion people use the core Facebook app, but also more than 700 million people use Groups, and 700 million use WhatsApp, and 600 million use Messenger, and more than 300 million people use Instagram every month. Now, we're building this family so we can offer unique, world-class experiences for all of the ways that people want to share.

—F8, March 25, 2015

THE BASIC THEORY that we have is that there are a small number of services that are going to be ubiquitous utilities that 1 billion or 2 billion or more people are going to want to use. So that's core basic messaging, the core functionality around having your real identity and connecting with all of your real friends and family online. Those are things that we just think are just going to be ubiquitous. So we want to build those.

—**quarterly earnings call, April 7, 2016**

WE DON'T NEED to get any lawyers involved. Let's just talk alone.

—**line to leaders whose companies he's interested in acquiring,** *New York Times*, **May 12, 2012**

I CAN'T SEE at any point us getting into producing our own content. I just think there are so many other people who produce awesome content that that's just not our place, but we're going to keep on getting better and better at ranking and showing the more relevant content and giving people the tools that they need to share exactly what they want.

—Atlantic Live, September 18, 2013

MOBILE IS A huge opportunity for Facebook. Our goal is to connect everyone in the world. And over the next 5 years, we expect 4 billion to 5 billion people to have smartphones. That's more than twice as many people that have computers today. So building great services for these devices is essential for us to help people connect. We also think that people are inherently social, and having a device with you wherever you are creates more opportunities for sharing and connecting.

—Seeking Alpha, July 26, 2012

FACEBOOK IS A mobile company. As I've said before, there are three main parts of our strategy; build the best mobile products, build the platform and services that leverage the social graph, and build a really strong monetization effort engine.

—quarterly earnings call, January 30, 2013

WE AGREE, STALKING isn't cool; but being able to know what's going on in your friends' lives is. This is information people used to dig for on a daily basis, nicely reorganized and summarized so people can learn about the people they care about. None of your information is visible to anyone who couldn't see it before the changes.

—on its controversial feature News Feed, when a user termed it "just too creepy, too stalker-esque, and a feature that has to go," Facebook blog, September 5, 2006

UNTIL RECENTLY, THERE hasn't been a good system for you to keep in touch with all of the other people who are in your life who you meet at some point who are important or were important and you want to keep up with, but you don't have a way to talk to on a day to day basis, and you wouldn't go out of your way to call, and you would never sit down with them in person. It's the power that's unlocked from that is what we're seeing here.

When you can build up the value of all of those latent connections and keep them open, this is the type of stuff that becomes possible. But it's because they want to do it on their own anyway; we're just allowing people the ability to do those things.

—Computer History Museum, July 21, 2010

PEOPLE DON'T MOSTLY use [Facebook] for replacing the face-to-face interactions that they have. It's for making it so that you can communicate with people who you wouldn't otherwise have the opportunity to connect with.

—Townhall Q&A in Rome, Italy, August 29, 2016

[FACEBOOK IS] ESSENTIALLY an online directory for students. Where people can go and look up other people and find relevant information about them. Everything from what they're interested in, to their contact information, what courses they're taking, who they know, who their friends are, what people say about them, what photos they have now. I guess it's mostly [a] utility for people to figure out just what's going on in their lives and in their friends' lives for people they care about.

—Entrepreneurial Thought Leaders Seminars,
Stanford, 2005

THERE HAS BEEN a lot of speculation reporting that fewer teens are using Facebook. But based on our data, that just isn't true. It's difficult to measure this perfectly, since some young people lied of their age. But based on the best data we have, we believe that we're close to fully penetrated in the US teen demographic for a while and the number of teens using Facebook on both a daily and monthly basis has been steady over the past year and half.

—quarterly earnings call, July 24, 2013

PEOPLE SHARE AND put billions of connections into this big graph every day. . . . We want to, you know, over the next five or 10 years, really take on a road map to try to understand, you know, everything in the world semantically, and kind of map everything out. And we want to play a role in helping, you know, people build companies and create jobs and build a knowledge economy.

—TechCrunch Disrupt, September 11, 2013

FROM THE BEGINNING, Facebook hasn't been about building a website. Facebook is about all of the people using it and all of the things that are important to you.

—Facebook blog, July 15, 2009

WHETHER IN TIMES of tragedy or joy, people want to share and help one another. This human need is what inspires us to continue to innovate and build things that allow people to connect easily and share their lives with one another.

—Facebook blog, February 4, 2010

OUR PHILOSOPHY IS that people own their information and control who they share it with. When a person shares information on Facebook, they first need to grant Facebook a license to use that information so that we can show it to other people they've asked us to share it with. Without this license, we couldn't help people share that information.

—Facebook blog, February 16, 2009

SIX YEARS AGO, we built Facebook around a few simple ideas. People want to share and stay connected with their friends and the people around them. If we give people control over what they share, they will want to share more. If people share more, the world will become more open and connected. And a world that's more open and connected is a better world. These are still our core principles today.

—*Washington Post,* May 24, 2010

THE CHALLENGE IS how a network like ours facilitates sharing and innovation, offers control and choice, and makes this experience easy for everyone. These are issues we think about all the time. Whenever we make a change, we try to apply the lessons we've learned along the way. The biggest message we have heard recently is that people want easier control over their information. Simply put, many of you thought our controls were too complex. Our intention was to give you lots of granular controls; but that may not have been what many of you wanted. We just missed the mark.

—*Washington Post*, May 24, 2010

THE REAL QUESTION for me is, do people have the tools that they need in order to make those decisions well? And I think that it's actually really important that Facebook continually makes it easier and easier to make those decisions.... If people feel like they don't have control over how they're sharing things, then we're failing them.

—*Charlie Rose*, November 7, 2011

I FOUNDED FACEBOOK on the idea that people want to share and connect with people in their lives, but to do this everyone needs complete control over who they share with at all times.

This idea has been the core of Facebook since day one. When I built the first version of Facebook, almost nobody I knew wanted a public page on the Internet. That seemed scary. But as long as they could make their page private, they felt safe sharing with their friends online. Control was key. With Facebook, for the first time, people had the tools they needed to do this. That's how Facebook became the world's biggest community online. We made it easy for people to feel comfortable sharing things about their real lives.

—Facebook blog, November 29, 2011

EARLY ON, WE wanted to establish this culture of real identity on the service. And, you know, there weren't really any other online services or communities where people were openly their real self before that.

—Startup School, October 20, 2012

IF YOUR FRIENDS all call you by a nickname and you want to use that name on Facebook, you should be able to do that. In this way, we should be able to support everyone using their own real names, including everyone in the transgender community.

—Facebook comment, June 30, 2015

I THINK THAT these companies with those big ad networks are basically getting away with collecting huge amounts of information. . . . But I think because people can see how much information people are sharing about themselves on Facebook, it appears scarier.

—*Charlie Rose*, November 7, 2011

WE DO NOT give advertisers data when they are advertising in our system. . . . The way that it works is that advertisers tell us what they want to target, and then we try, within our system, to show the best content, including ads, to the people who are going to find it the most relevant and are within the targeting.

—**Atlantic Live, September 18, 2013**

SO FOR THE next five or 10 years the question isn't going to be, does Facebook get to 2 billion or 3 billion? I mean, that's obviously one question. But the bigger question is, what services can get built now that every company can assume they can get access to knowing who everyone's friends are.

—*Bloomberg Businessweek*, **October 4, 2012**

A LOT OF people increasingly seem to equate an advertising business model with somehow being out of alignment with your customers. I think it's the most ridiculous concept. What, you think because you're paying Apple that you're somehow in alignment with them? If you were in alignment with them, then they'd make their products a lot cheaper!

—*Time*, December 15, 2014

WE WANT THE organic content to be of the same basic type of formats as paid content.

—quarterly earnings call, January 30, 2013

IF WE ARE doing our job well, then people will come to Facebook to consume a lot of content. If people don't connect to the advertising content, then it's not good for anyone. It's not good for the people using Facebook, it's not good for the advertisers, and then ultimately we don't make money.

—*Vanity Fair*, April 3, 2013

The question isn't "What do we want to know about people?" It's "What do people want to tell about themselves?"

—*Charlie Rose*, November 7, 2011

CREATING CHANNELS BETWEEN people
who want to work together towards change
has always been one of the ways that social
movements push the world forward and make it
better. Both U.S. President Barack Obama and
French President Nicholas Sarkozy have used
Facebook as a way to organize their supporters.
From the protests against the Columbian FARC,
a 40-year-old terrorist organization, to fighting
oppressive, fringe groups in India, people use
Facebook as a platform to build connections and
organize action.

—Facebook blog, April 8, 2009

FACEBOOK WANTS TO . . . turn the lonely,
antisocial world of random chance into a friendly
world, a serendipitous world. You'll be working
and living inside a network of people, and you'll
never have to be alone again. The Internet, and
the whole world, will feel more like a family, or a
college dorm, or an office where your co-workers
are also your best friends.

—*Time*, December 27, 2010/January 3, 2011

THE REASON WHY we're so excited about [Facebook Live] is that it's this new really raw, personal, and spontaneous way that people can share, right, where now you don't have to take a bunch of videos or photos and curate them and find exactly the most perfect one. You can just go live and feel like you're really there with your friends or people all over the world.

—Facebook Live video, April 9, 2016

WE VIEW THE social space as almost this matrix. You can think about it as a two-dimensional grid where one axis is the richness of the content that people want to share, and the other axis is the size of the audience, or intimacy of how people want to share.

—quarterly earnings call, October 8, 2015

I THINK THE basic idea here is that there is a phenomenon in people's interaction. The message that you get, in a lot of ways, is actually less important than who you get it from. It you get it from someone that you trust a lot more, then you really listen to it, whereas if you get it from someone you don't trust, you might actually believe the opposite of what they said because you don't trust them. I think that's the basis of value that people get on the site. I go to someone's profile and see that they like this band. That means more to me than if I just saw a billboard for that band. We figured that in the really organic way to make money and sustain the company, that these interests would be aligned.

—*Fast Company*, September 17, 2009

Process

If you believe something must be fully perfect just to get started, a lot of the time you'll never get started.

—*Wired*, November 10, 2016

[COMPUTER CODING, LIKE journalism, is] iterative, right? You'll write it, then next year you'll write another story, and another, and eventually, the story will be the way you want it.

—*Fast Company*, March 19, 2012

NO ONE STARTS off knowing everything that they're going to need to build something. So the best thing that you can do is not study as much as you can before, or not pretend that you know everything. It's go into it with this mindset that your job is to learn as much as you can as quickly as you can.

—Townhall Q&A in Rome, Italy, August 29, 2016

My experience is that people often shy away from hard decisions for longer than they should because they are worried about some bad effect. People talk about, oh this is going to hurt in the short term but help in the long run, right? And my experience is that the long run always happens sooner than you think.

—*Fast Company*, April 11, 2017

I would like Facebook to always operate as fast as a company that's 10 times smaller than we are.

—*Bloomberg Businessweek*, October 4, 2012

We've changed our internal motto from "Move fast and break things" to "Move fast with stable infrastructure."

—*Wired*, April 30, 2014

By building a stable infrastructure, we allow ourselves to always make sure that we're moving forward, even if we move a little bit slower upfront. Because when you build something that you don't have to fix it 10 times, you can move forward on top of what you've built.

—*Wired*, April 30, 2014

A LOT OF people think that innovation is just having your great idea. But a lot of it is just moving quickly and trying a lot of things. So at Facebook we've really built our whole company and our whole culture around that. We do things like shift code every single day. And we have this tradition of having hackathons which are events where all of our engineers, and really the whole company, get together and stay up just all night building things, whatever they want, not just what they're doing for work, just trying things out and innovating.

—*Fast Company*: 30 Second MBA, March 2, 2012

WE HAVE A saying: "nothing at Facebook is someone else's problem." If you see something wrong, you go fix it.

—Facebook Community Summit, June 22, 2017

I DON'T GET to write a lot of code in Facebook's code base anymore. We have a rule that if you make a change you have to support your change, so if it breaks you have to drop whatever you're doing to fix it. I feel like I'd kind of be a jerk if I made some other engineer go fix my change at Facebook, so I kind of gave up on coding within the Facebook system.

—**Techonomy, November 11, 2016**

ON A DAY-TO-DAY basis, a lot of the decisions that I'm making are like, "OK, is this going to destroy the company? Because, if not, then let them test it."

—*Masters of Scale*, **May 25, 2017**

OUR JOB IS to stay focused on building the best service for [third-party social applications]. And if we do that, then there's a massive market and a lot of value to be built in the world. And if we don't, then someone else will do it.

—*Fast Company*, July 6, 2011

FOR US, PRODUCTS don't really get that interesting to turn into businesses until they have about 1 billion people using them.

—quarterly earnings call, October 28, 2014

WE HAVE THIS concept of serendipity—humans do. A lucky coincidence. ... When you have this kind of context of what's going on, it's just going to make people's lives richer, because instead of missing 99% of them, maybe now you'll start seeing a lot more of them.

—*Time*, December 27, 2010/January 3, 2011

I think a simple rule of business is, if you do the things that are easier first, then you can actually make a lot of progress.

—*Charlie Rose*, November 7, 2011

THE WHOLE COMPANY is really optimized around someone joining, being able to build something very quickly, be able to launch it quickly, iterate very quickly on that. Get feedback quickly. That moving fast ethos is a huge part of what we do. … And we have this belief that you never build something great by doing the same way that other people have done it. … For the core things that we wanna do, when we have the decision to either do it the same way that someone else has done it or do it a different way, we're gonna choose to do it in a different way. And we really encourage people all throughout the company to think about things in that way and make bolder decisions.

—*Business Insider*, October 14, 2010

ONE OF OUR values is "move fast." That means you should be able to come here and build an app faster than you can anywhere else, including on your own.

—**Facebook post, December 19, 2016**

CAN WE TAKE what used to take 10 clicks for someone to get the information they need and reduce it to three? It saves time over thousands of operations. What can we do with that time?

—*Fast Company*, **March 19, 2012**

WHEN WE SAY "hacker," there's this whole definition that engineers have for themselves where it's very much a compliment when you call someone a hacker, where to hack something means to build something very quickly, right? In one night, you can sit down and you can churn out a lot of code, and at the end, you have a product.

—*60 Minutes*, **December 1, 2010**

WE WANT TO make sure that everyone can come and add their ideas. I mean, some of the best ideas throughout the company's evolution, they have just been from just places all throughout the company, whether it's an engineer or someone on the customer support team or just different areas around the company. So we've always had these hackathons that are basically time that we allocate that, the only rule is that you don't work on what you work on the rest of the time. It's basically an incubator for people to prototype different ideas, much in the spirit of how Facebook got founded originally. You can build anything good in a day, or a couple of days . . . and get a version of that running.

—*Business Insider*, October 14, 2010

WE HAVE THIS saying at Facebook that code wins arguments.... You can talk about something for a long time, and I think in a lot of places you talk about stuff for years ... and then finally someone goes and builds a version of it, and that's actually how you make progress in the world, right? So it's not just sitting around and talking about an idea, it's actually who can sit down and code a version that works, even if it's not the perfect version right away.

—Facebook Live video, August 2, 2016

YOU'D ACTUALLY BE surprised how much of the product road map over time is set, not just by us kind of talking about what we think we should do and deciding, but from engineers coming up with ideas, showing them, and then eventually that makes its way onto the road map of what we want to build.

—Facebook Live video, December 5, 2016

One definition that I have for a good team is a group of people that makes better decisions as a whole than would individually make.

—Startup School, October 25, 2013

You should never hire someone to work for you unless you would work for them.

—*Masters of Scale*, May 25, 2017

CERTAINLY HAVING PEOPLE go work in a silent office will allow them to focus more on whatever task they are doing. That is kind of without a doubt. So the reason why I think having people work in an open floor plan is a better idea is that you collaborate more and you understand what the direction is that you need to go in better.

—Townhall Q&A at Facebook, September 15, 2015

EVERYONE HAS A desk [in the open office], even the people who are running the company. There's no kind of special offices or anything like that.

—Facebook Live video, September 14, 2015

Part III

A LEGACY IN THE MAKING

Mission

THIS IS OUR challenge. We have to build a world where every single person has a sense of purpose and community. That's how we'll bring the world closer together.

—Facebook Community Summit, June 22, 2017

A LOT OF the best things that happen aren't because some engineer in California started building something, but they start with someone somewhere who has an idea and is passionate about it and does what they need to do to make it real.

—Facebook Social Good Forum, November 29, 2017

Finding your purpose isn't enough. The challenge for our generation is creating a world where everyone has a sense of purpose.

—Harvard commencement address, May 25, 2017

THE THING THAT we need to do is make sure
that we're giving everyone around the world . . .
the tools they need to push for the change they
want to see.

—North Carolina A&T State University, March 13, 2017

IF WE HAVE 2 billion people who use Facebook,
then why are only 100 million of them in
meaningful groups? Why aren't we doing a better
job of connecting more people to meaningful
groups? So that, now, is the whole thrust of what
I want our company to focus on.

—University of Kansas, November 10, 2017

ONE OF THE questions that I asked our team is, can we help people connect with, maybe like, people you should know? Right? A mentor or a teacher. There's a lot of data that suggests that if you have just one teacher, right, or parent, or mentor who can help raise your sights on what you achieve that makes a really big impact.

—**University of Kansas, November 10, 2017**

FACEBOOK IS FREE. It always will be. This is part of our mission, to make it so that we can build a global community so that everyone can be a part of it.

—**Facebook Live video, June 14, 2016**

YOU REALIZE A billion is sort of an arbitrary number. Our mission isn't to connect a billion people, it's to connect everyone in the world.

—*Vanity Fair*, **September 8, 2015**

ONE OF THE things that we need in our society is a digital social fabric. And I think we can be a part of that.

—**Atlantic Live, September 18, 2013**

CHINA, THAT IS a more complex situation. Obviously, you can't have a mission of wanting to connect everyone in the world and leave out the biggest country. So over the long-term, that is a situation that we will need to try to figure out a way forward on.

—**quarterly earnings call, October 8, 2015**

WHEN I STARTED Facebook, the mission of connecting people wasn't a controversial thing. The default assumption was that the world was coming closer together. But for the last couple of years, it's really been much more of a question.

—***Wired*, February 16, 2017**

A LOT OF folks just wish that if we can turn down the temperature a little bit on some of the divisive debates, then there actually is more common ground than you might hear a lot of time in the news, just based on what we all care about in our local communities.

—**University of Kansas, November 10, 2017**

WE NEED TO give people a voice to get a diversity of opinions out there, but we also need to build enough common ground so we can all make progress together. We need to stay connected with people we already know and care about, but we also need to meet new people with new perspectives. We need support from family and friends, but we also need to build communities to support us as well.

—**Facebook Community Summit, June 22, 2017**

OUR GOAL MUST be to help people see a more complete picture, not just alternate perspectives. We must be careful how we do this. Research shows that some of the most obvious ideas, like showing people an article from the opposite perspective, actually deepen polarization by framing other perspectives as foreign. A more effective approach is to show a range of perspectives, let people see where their views are on a spectrum and come to a conclusion on what they think is right.

—Building Global Community letter,
February 16, 2017

RESEARCH SUGGESTS THE best solutions for improving discourse may come from getting to know each other as whole people instead of just opinions—something Facebook may be uniquely suited to do.

—Building Global Community letter,
February 16, 2017

OUR PHILOSOPHY IS to give the most voice to the most people, not that everyone can say everything. I don't think we will be the ones to mark things as false. Our approach is to try to get community to do it and I would rather that it come from community rather than us.

—*Recode*, February 16, 2017

WE NEED TO be careful not to discourage sharing of opinions or to mistakenly restrict accurate content. We do not want to be arbiters of truth ourselves, but instead rely on our community and trusted third parties.

—Facebook post, November 18, 2016

WE CAN'T CREATE a culture that says it cares about diversity and then excludes almost half the country because they back a political candidate. There are many reasons a person might support Trump that do not involve racism, sexism, xenophobia or accepting sexual assault. It may be because they believe strongly in smaller government, a different tax policy, health care system, religious issues, gun rights or any other issue where he disagrees with Hillary.

—internal Facebook memo

SILICON VALLEY HAS a reputation for being liberal. But the Facebook community includes more than 1.6 billion people of every background and ideology—from liberal to conservative and everything in between.

We've built Facebook to be a platform for all ideas. Our community's success depends on everyone feeling comfortable sharing anything they want. It doesn't make sense for our mission or our business to suppress political content or prevent anyone from seeing what matters most to them.

—Facebook post, May 18, 2016

SOME PEOPLE HAVE asked for a "dislike" button because they want to be able to say "That thing isn't good." That's not something we think is good for the world.

—*Esquire*, September 23, 2015

OUR LIVES ARE all connected. In the next generation, our greatest opportunities and challenges we can only take on together— ending poverty, curing disease, stopping climate change, spreading freedom and tolerance, stopping terrorism. No single group or even country can do that alone.

—Facebook Community Summit, June 22, 2017

THE PRODUCT DIRECTIVE that I've given to all of our teams is to shift from focusing on showing the most meaningful content to people to instead now encouraging the most meaningful social interaction.

—quarterly earnings call, January 31, 2018

WE HAVE THIS News Feed quality panel where we actually have thousands of people who come in, and we show them News Feed stories and ask them to rank them themselves. That way we have a sense of what sort of a ground-truth quality is that people care about.

—Techonomy, November 11, 2016

THE MEDIA DIVERSITY, and diversity of information, that you're getting through a social system like Facebook is going to be inherently more diverse than what you would have gotten from watching one of the three news stations and having that be your newspaper, or your TV station, 20 years ago.

—Techonomy, November 11, 2016

For important missions, the more you learn, the more you find needs to be done.

—Tsinghua University, October 24, 2015

BUILDING A MISSION and building a business go hand in hand. And it is definitely true that the primary thing that makes me excited about what we're doing is the mission, but I also think that from the very beginning, we've had this healthy understanding, which is that we need to do both.

—TechCrunch Disrupt, September 11, 2012

I AM MUCH more motivated by making sure that we have the biggest impact on the world than by building a business or making sure we don't fail.

—*Masters of Scale*, May 25, 2017

OUR GOAL IS not to build a platform—it's to be across all of them.

—*Charlie Rose*, November 7, 2011

I'M HERE TO build something for the long term. Anything else is a distraction.

—*Fast Company*, May 1, 2007

I THINK THAT people focus way too much on competitors and not enough on their own execution. And I think if we just do a good job executing, then that to me is by far the biggest variable in what we achieve.

—*Business Insider*, February 28, 2016

[STEVE JOBS] WAS amazing. I had a lot of questions for him on . . . how to build a team around you that's focused on building as high quality and good things as you are. How to keep an organization focused, when I think the tendency for larger companies is to try to fray and go into all these different areas. Yeah, I mean a lot just on the aesthetics and kind of mission orientation of companies. Apple is a company that is so focused on just building products that—for their customers and their users—it's such a deep part of their mission [to] build these beautiful products for their users. And I think we connected a lot on this level.

Facebook has this mission that's really more than just trying to build a company that has a market cap or a value. It's like we're trying to do this thing in the world. I just think we connected on that level.

—*Charlie Rose*, November 7, 2011

Values

I'm of the belief that values are only useful when they're controversial.

—TechCrunch Disrupt, September 11, 2013

IF A TECHNOLOGY doesn't actually help us socially understand each other better, it isn't going to catch on and succeed.

—*Business Insider*, February 28, 2016

OPTIMISTS TEND TO be successful, and pessimists tend to be right. . . . If you think that something's going to be terrible and it's going to fail, then you're going to look for the data points that prove you right. And you'll find them! That's what pessimists do. But if you think that something is possible, then you're going to try to find a way to make it work.

—Facebook Social Good Forum, November 29, 2017

WHAT WE'RE DOING is really hard. And we think that we're better off focusing on this piece [building social networks]. I think that building a great game service is really hard. Building a great music service is really hard. Building a great movie service is really hard. And we just believe that an independent entrepreneur will always beat a division of a big company, which is why we think that the strategy of these other companies trying to do everything themselves will inevitably be less successful than an ecosystem where you have someone like Facebook trying to build the core product to help people connect and then independent great companies that are only focused on one or two things doing those things really well.

—*Charlie Rose*, November 7, 2011

So many businesses get worried about looking like they might make a mistake, they become afraid to take any risk. Companies are set up so that people judge each other on failure. I'm not going to get fired if we have a bad year. Or a bad five years. I don't have to worry about making things look good if they're not. I can actually set up the company to create value.

—*Fast Company*, March 19, 2012

I always kind of see how I want things to be better, and I'm generally not happy with how things are, or the level of service that we're providing for people, or the quality of the teams that we built. But if you look at this objectively, we're doing so well on so many of these things. I think it's important to have gratitude for that.

—*Bloomberg Businessweek*, January 30, 2014

THERE'S AN INTENSE focus on openness, sharing information, as both an ideal and a practical strategy to get things done.

—*Fast Company*, May 1, 2007

THEY [MICROSOFT] REALLY are the underdog here. They're incentivized to go out and innovate. When you're an incumbent in an area . . . there is tension between innovating and trying new things versus what you already have.

—on why Facebook chose to partner with Bing rather than Google, *Fast Company*, October 14, 2010

I GUESS WHAT it probably turns out is, other people didn't care as much as we did.

—*Time*, December 27, 2010/January 3, 2011

JUST BECAUSE A tool can be used for good and bad, that doesn't make the tool bad—it just means you need to understand what the negative is so that you can mitigate it.

—*New York Times*, January 11, 2018

THE WAY THAT people think about privacy is changing a bit. What people want isn't complete privacy. It isn't that they want secrecy. It's that they want control over what they share and what they don't.

—*Time*, May 20, 2010

WE ARE ACTUALLY a privacy innovation, right? We carved out this space and made it so that, for the first time ever, it was possible to share content with just the people you cared about.

—Townhall Q&A in Berlin, Germany, February 26, 2016

People trust people, not institutions.

—*Bloomberg Businessweek*, September 21, 2017

ONE [QUALITY THAT makes good entrepreneurs and CEOs] is just having a really strong sense of what you want to do, because along the way there are so many distractions that if you're not completely clear on what you want to do, you're going to get sidetracked. That's number one: being clear about what you want to do, and really caring about it.

Number two is building a good team. That's what I spend a huge amount of time on. When I'm not building products—I work with teams to build products—so it goes all the way down the organization from really good head of engineering and getting the best hackers and engineers and people who want to build stuff, to the head of product who can really communicate exactly what you're going to do, and make sure that every person in the company knows what the plan is, to really good business folks like [Facebook's COO] Sheryl [Sandberg]. . . .

Should I run the company or not? If I were to disappear, any of them could run the company. If you have a clear idea of what you're doing and you have great people, then that's a lot of the battle.

—Computer History Museum, July 21, 2010

THE US GOVERNMENT should be the champion
for the internet, not a threat. They need to be
much more transparent about what they're
doing, or otherwise people will believe the worst.

—Facebook post, March 13, 2014

SO WE HAD this episode where Yahoo and
Viacom and all these companies were trying to
buy the company. And it was this really kind of
crazy time. Because we started the company as
a dorm room project.... It was [a] really pivotal
point for us, because when you're 22 and have
an opportunity to sell something for that much
money, you reach this point where, like, you're
not making decisions to maximize the amount of
money that you're making. Where I mean, like,
any amount of money would not be worth the,
like, the last few years that we've spent building
up the company.

—press conference, May 28, 2010

WE'VE ALWAYS BEEN significantly smaller per employee compared to the number of people who we serve in the world. So it's really baked into the company that we have to build systems and software that take into account the leverage that employees here have. And that's actually one of the reasons why a lot of people love working here and one of the biggest reasons why people cite for wanting to join the company and staying here. So it's also affected the strategy. I mentioned we believe that all these consumer products, and maybe even more than consumer products that people use, will become social over time.

—Seeking Alpha, July 26, 2012

I'VE ALWAYS FOCUSED on a couple of things....
One is having a clear direction for the company
and what we build. And the other is just trying
to build the best team possible toward that.... I
think, as a company, if you can just get those two
things right—having a clear direction on what
you are trying to do, and bringing in great people
who can execute on the stuff—then you can do
pretty well.

—D8 Conference, 2010

I DON'T THINK of myself as a businessperson. I just think that one of the things that's amazing about the Internet is if you build something good that is a service that is valuable for people, it can spread quickly and if you create value for other people, then you might be able to realize a portion of that value yourself. I never thought about Facebook as starting a business that would grow its own value, but in a way I think it's really good that the world works this way.... [I]f someone does something that's valuable that that's enough to build a good business.... I don't think that I've focused on a lot of the same things that a lot of other businesspeople do, but every day we try to come in and build the best product for people.

—*Time*, 2010

WE DO TRY to attract people, but our goal isn't necessarily to keep people forever. Some companies are really good at training people. A lot of people for a long time went to IBM because it was great to learn sales. We want Facebook to be one of the best places people can go to learn how to build stuff. If you want to build a company, nothing's better than jumping in and trying to build one. But Facebook is also great for entrepreneurs/hackers. If people want to come for a few years and move on and build something great, that's something we're proud of. Steve Chen when he started working on YouTube was working on Facebook. They left, did something cool. I'm not encouraging people working at Facebook to leave. We're not pretending that we're building a company that hackers would want to stay at forever.

—Startup School, October 29, 2011

BUILDING A COMPANY is one of the most efficient ways in the world that you can kind of align the incentives of a lot of smart people towards making a change.

—Startup School, October 29, 2011

THERE'S SO MUCH research that shows that you need diverse teams to do the best work. So it's important that we do better on diversity, not only because it's the right thing to do for the country and for people, but because that's the only way that we're going to serve our community the best.

—North Carolina A&T State University, March 13, 2017

IN MY LIFE, the people I've learned from most
are the people I do my work with every day. It's a
real issue and it will hold back progress if women
don't have the same opportunities to learn from
the people around them.

—Facebook post, February 6, 2018

THE TWO THINGS that you focus on are
maintaining what you have now that's good
and growing.... Focusing on things that are
sustainable and skill-able, and so that when we
launched more skills, or go on to the next market,
we are going to set ourselves up to have the same
success we've had without hurting ourselves in
the current position. It's basically maintaining
the utility while growing.

—Entrepreneurial Thought Leaders Seminars,
Stanford, 2005

THE MOST IMPORTANT thing that we should be
doing as a business is prioritizing, figuring out
what the right things are for us to be approaching
now. ... [W]orking on stuff that's really
important now is always like the best use of our
time.

—**Entrepreneurial Thought Leaders Seminars,
Stanford, 2005**

THE TWO MOST important things that I look
for [when hiring employees] are, number one,
raw intelligence; I think that that's the most
important thing that I look for. And the second:
just alignment with what we're trying to do.
People can be really smart, or have skills that are
directly applicable, but if they don't really believe
in it, then they are not going to really work hard.

—**Entrepreneurial Thought Leaders Seminars,
Stanford, 2005**

THE DEMANDS AND the amount of work it takes
to put something like [Facebook] into place, it's
just so much that if you weren't completely into
what you were doing and you didn't think it was
an important thing, then it would be irrational to
spend that much time on it. ... People constantly
try to put us in a bucket: are we trying to sell the
company? What are we trying to do? What is the
business strategy? ... Whereas for me and a lot of
people around me, that's not really what we focus
on. We're just focused on building things.

—*Time*, July 17, 2007

I don't really know what the next big thing is because I don't spend my time making big things. I spend time making small things and then when the time comes I put them together.

—*Harvard Crimson*, June 10, 2004

WE CAN ALWAYS be innovating more, doing more things. ... I'm just an impatient person, right. I want to see us, like, release all these products very quickly, and—and that's like—that's a big thing for—for our company. We love moving fast, and being bold, and kind of making those big things.

—*ABC World News*, July 21, 2010

IF YOU DON'T want to sell your company, don't get into a process where you're talking to people about selling your company.

—*New York Times*, May 12, 2012

I WOULD BE a little careful about a company like ours trying too hard to change the laws in any country. We're here to serve people and the laws that they've chosen to have for themselves more than try to influence that.

—**Q&A with the media in India, October 9, 2014**

THE PROBLEM IS that if you break the law
[regulating speech] in a country, then oftentimes
that country will just block the whole service
entirely . . . which then makes it so that millions
of people are now deprived of the tools that they
were using to communicate with their friends
and their family and to express as much as
possible.

—Townhall Q&A in Bogotá, Colombia,
January 14, 2015

AS A JEW, my parents taught me that we must
stand up against attacks on all communities.
Even if an attack isn't against you today, in
time attacks on freedom for anyone will hurt
everyone.

—Facebook post, December 9, 2015

YOU'VE PROBABLY SEEN the story about Ahmed, the 14 year old student in Texas who built a clock and was arrested when he took it to school.

Having the skill and ambition to build something cool should lead to applause, not arrest. The future belongs to people like Ahmed.

Ahmed, if you ever want to come by Facebook, I'd love to meet you. Keep building.

—Facebook post, September 16, 2015

THERE IS NO place for hate in our community. That's why we've always taken down any post that promotes or celebrates hate crimes or acts of terrorism—including what happened in Charlottesville [Virginia]. With the potential for more rallies, we're watching the situation closely and will take down threats of physical harm.

—Facebook post, August 16, 2017

DIAMOND REYNOLDS WENT live on Facebook immediately after her fiancé, Philando Castile, had been shot by police in his car. Philando later died from his wounds. In the video, Diamond's 4-year-old daughter is watching from the back seat.... While I hope we never have to see another video like Diamond's, it reminds us why coming together to build a more open and connected world is so important—and how far we still have to go.

—**Facebook post, July 7, 2016**

WE BELIEVE A lot in transparency and giving people a voice, right? And if we're not going to give [the police] body cameras, then we'll give everyone a [Facebook] Live camera.

—**North Carolina A&T State University,**
March 13, 2017

IT SEEMS LIKE a good time to say thank you to all the journalists around the world who work tirelessly and sometimes put their lives in danger to surface the truth.

I don't always agree with everything you say, but that's how democracy is supposed to work.

—**Facebook post, February 20, 2017**

KNOWLEDGE ECONOMIES HAVE the productive property, which is that me knowing something doesn't prevent you from knowing it, right? So the more information that you share, the more informed everyone is, the better ideas can generally spread. If you have an idea I can benefit from that, and it ends up being positive sum.

—**Atlantic Live, September 18, 2013**

UNDERSTANDING THE WORLD means helping people not just share day-to-day updates, but also building up long-term knowledge about the world and being able to answer questions for you that no other service can.

—quarterly earnings call, October 30, 2013

OPPORTUNITY IS CERTAINLY not equally distributed right now. And so, one of the big questions is why. And one of the things that I found really striking this year is that it's often the relationships and social capital that you have that make a bigger difference than what you know.

—University of Kansas, November 10, 2017

MY WIFE IS a doctor and she always tells me about examples of things that you don't think of as traditionally contagious diseases but that actually are highly correlated in social networks—happiness, smoking, obesity, things like that. I mean, happiness isn't a disease but they're actually highly correlated. So it seems like there's something about social networks that should be factored into health care and keeping people healthy that just isn't today.

—*Bloomberg Businessweek*, October 4, 2012

TODAY, WE HAVE a level of wealth inequality that hurts everyone. When you don't have the freedom to take your idea and turn it into a historic enterprise, we all lose. Right now our society is way over-indexed on rewarding success and we don't do nearly enough to make it easy for everyone to take lots of shots.

—Harvard commencement address, May 25, 2017

IF WE WANT everyone in the world to have access to all the opportunities that come with the internet, we need to keep the internet free and open.

—Facebook post, July 12, 2017

OUR LIVES ARE connected, and whether we're welcoming a refugee fleeing war or an immigrant seeking new opportunity, whether we're coming together to fight global disease like ebola or to address climate change, I hope that we have the courage to see that the path forward is to bring people together, not push people apart.

—F8, April 12, 2016

WITHDRAWING FROM THE Paris climate agreement is bad for the environment, bad for the economy, and it puts our children's future at risk.

For our part, we've committed that every new data center we build will be powered by 100% renewable energy.

Stopping climate change is something we can only do as a global community, and we have to act together before it's too late.

—Facebook post, June 1, 2017

THE AMOUNT OF power that's required for all of the Facebook infrastructure to deliver Facebook for you for a year is less than the energy that it takes to make one cup of coffee.

—Facebook Live video, February 25, 2016

Accountability

THE REASON OUR community exists today is not because we avoided mistakes. It's because we believe what we're doing matters enough to keep trying to solve our greatest challenges—knowing full well that we'll fail again and again, but that it's the only way to make progress.

—Facebook post, February 4, 2018

I ALWAYS MAKE a point, when I think that people are being too nice to us, they're writing too nice of stuff about us, to get up in front of the company and say, "Hey, we're not as good as they say we are now," and then when I think that people are being too critical, underestimating us, saying, "You know, I think we're not as bad as they say we are either."

—TechCrunch Disrupt, September 11, 2012

EVERYTHING I DO breaks, but we fix it quickly.

—TechCrunch Disrupt, September 11, 2012

WE REALLY MESSED this one up. When we launched News Feed and Mini-Feed we were trying to provide you with a stream of information about your social world. Instead, we did a bad job of explaining what the new features were and an even worse job of giving you control of them. I'd like to correct those errors now. . . . This may sound silly, but I want to thank all of you who have written in and created groups and protested. Even though I wish I hadn't made so many of you angry, I am glad we got to hear you. And I am also glad that News Feed highlighted all these groups so people could find them and share their opinions with each other as well.

—Facebook blog, September 8, 2006

We view it as our job to protect all of the people who use Facebook and their information, and it's the government's job to protect us all in a broader sense, in terms of safety and [to] protect our rights.

—Atlantic Live, September 18, 2013

I actually am not sure we shouldn't be regulated. You know, I think in general technology is an increasingly important trend in the world, and I actually think the question is more what is the right regulation, rather than yes or no, should it be regulated?

—CNN Money, March 21, 2018

ON THE BASIC side, you know, there are things like ads transparency regulation that I would love to see, right? If you look at how much regulation there is around advertising on TV and print, you know, it's just not clear why there should be less on the internet, right? You should have the same level of transparency required.

—CNN Money, March 21, 2018

LAST QUARTER, WE made changes to show fewer viral videos to make sure people's time is well spent. In total, we made changes that reduced time spent on Facebook by roughly 50 million hours every day. By focusing on meaningful connections, our community and business will be stronger over the long term.

—Facebook post, January 31, 2018

WHEN WE USE social media to connect with people, that correlates with long term measures of well-being you'd expect, like happiness and health. But passively watching videos or reading articles may not have those same effects.

—Facebook post, January 31, 2018

WE'RE TRYING TO help push forward new formats that are not just about consuming content but are really about interacting, so Live, 360 video, and there will be others in the future.

—quarterly earnings call, April 27, 2016

WE'VE SEEN PEOPLE hurting themselves and others on Facebook—either live or in video posted later. It's heartbreaking, and I've been reflecting on how we can do better for our community.

If we're going to build a safe community, we need to respond quickly. We're working to make these videos easier to report so we can take the right action sooner—whether that's responding quickly when someone needs help or taking a post down.

—Facebook post, May 3, 2017

WE'VE ALSO BUILT new technology to detect suicidal posts that has helped first responders reach more than 100 people who needed help quickly, and we've built AI systems to flag suspicious behavior around elections in real time and remove terrorist content.

—Facebook post, January 31, 2018

I THINK A lot of people think about what we do as media, right, because the main product that most people use is News Feed.... But the reality is ... we're not a content company. We're not making that. We're a technology company which is building this really big infrastructure around the world.

—**Facebook Live video, February 25, 2016**

WHILE WE DON'T write the news stories you read and share, we also recognize we're more than just a distributor of news. We're a new kind of platform for public discourse—and that means we have a new kind of responsibility to enable people to have the most meaningful conversations, and to build a space where people can be informed.

—**Facebook post, December 15, 2016**

SOCIAL MEDIA AND, to some degree, online news in general, are short form and there are some positives, because it forces people to focus their message. But there are negatives too. If all you have is a short message, you tend to oversimplify and you remove the nuance.

—*Recode*, February 16, 2017

IF YOU'D TOLD me in 2004 when I was getting started with Facebook that a big part of my responsibility today would be to help protect the integrity of elections against interference by other governments, you know, I wouldn't have really believed that that was gonna be something that I would have to work on 14 years later.

—**CNN Money, March 21, 2018**

PERSONALLY I THINK the idea that fake news
on Facebook, of which it's a very small amount
of the content, influenced the election in any
way, I think is a pretty crazy idea. Voters make
decisions based on their lived experience.

—**Techonomy, November 11, 2016**

OVERALL, I AM proud of our role giving people
a voice in this [2016] election. We helped
more than 2 million people register to vote,
and based on our estimates we got a similar
number of people to vote who might have stayed
home otherwise. We helped millions of people
connect with candidates so they could hear from
them directly and be better informed. Most
importantly, we gave tens of millions of people
tools to share billions of posts and reactions
about this election. A lot of that dialog may not
have happened without Facebook.

—**Facebook post, November 12, 2016**

THE WORLD FEELS anxious and divided—and that played out on Facebook. We've seen abuse on our platform, including interference from nation states, the spread of news that is false, sensational and polarizing, and debate about the utility of social media. We have a responsibility to fully understand how our services are used, and to do everything we can to amplify the good and prevent harm.

—**Facebook post, January 31, 2018**

WE'RE REALLY AGAINST fake news and misinformation. There have been some accusations that say that, you know, we actually want this kind of content on our service because it's more content and people click on it. But that's crap. I mean, no one in our community wants fake information. Everyone wants real information. So, you know, if someone clicks on something and they have a bad experience, then they're not going to trust Facebook, and they're not going to want to get more content from Facebook, and that's not good for us.

—**North Carolina A&T State University, March 13, 2017**

Facebook's mission is all about giving people a voice and bringing people closer together. Those are deeply democratic values and we're proud of them. I don't want anyone to use our tools to undermine democracy. That's not what we stand for.

—Facebook post, September 21, 2017

WHAT WE SEE are a lot of folks trying to sow division, right? So that was a major tactic that we saw Russia try to use in the 2016 election. Actually, most of what they did was not directly, as far as we can tell from the data that we've seen, was not directly about the election, but was more about just dividing people. And, you know, so they'd run a group on, you know, for pro-immigration reform, and then they'd run another group against immigration reform, and just try to pit people against each other.

—CNN Money, March 21, 2018

THE INTEGRITY OF our elections is fundamental to democracy around the world. That's why we built teams dedicated to working on election integrity and preventing governments from interfering in the elections of other nations.

—Facebook Live video, September 21, 2017

IN 2016, WE were not as on top of a number of issues as we should've [been], whether it was Russian interference or fake news. But what we have seen since then is, you know, a number of months later there was a major French election, and there we deployed some AI tools that did a much better job of identifying Russian bots and basically Russian potential interference and weeding that out of the platform ahead of the election.

—CNN Money, March 21, 2018

I'VE DIRECTED OUR teams to invest so much in security—on top of the other investments we're making—that it will significantly impact our profitability going forward, and I wanted our investors to hear that directly from me. I believe this will make our society stronger and in doing so will be good for all of us over the long term.

—quarterly earnings call, November 1, 2017

THIS WAS A major breach of trust, and I'm really sorry that this happened. You know, we have a basic responsibility to protect people's data, and if we can't do that then we don't deserve to have the opportunity to serve people.

—on the Cambridge Analytica leak, CNN Money, March 21, 2018

OVERALL, I WOULD say that we're going through a broader philosophical shift in how we approach our responsibility as a company. For the first 10 or 12 years of the company, I viewed our responsibility as primarily building tools that, if we could put those tools in people's hands, then that would empower people to do good things. What I think we've learned now across a number of issues—not just data privacy, but also fake news and foreign interference in elections—is that we need to take a more proactive role and a broader view of our responsibility. It's not enough to just build tools. We need to make sure that they're used for good.

—testimony before the Senate Committee on the Judiciary and the Senate Committee on Commerce, Science, and Transportation, April 10, 2018

PEOPLE OFTEN ASK what the difference is between surveillance and what we do. And I think that the difference is extremely clear, which is that, on Facebook, you have control over your information. The content that you share, you put there. You can take it down at any time. The information that we collect, you can choose to have us not collect. You can delete any of it, and, of course, you can leave Facebook if you want. I know of no surveillance organization that gives people the option to delete the data that they have, or even know what—what they're collecting.

—testimony before the House of Representatives Energy and Commerce Committee, April 11, 2018

I'M THE FIRST to admit that we've made a bunch of mistakes.

—on FTC allegations of privacy violations, Facebook blog, November 29, 2011

Vision

YOU'RE NEVER GOING to get everything perfect, but every day you can come in and make progress and make people's lives, on balance, better. And if you repeat that process for a very long period of time, the value compounds and you can make a very big impact.

—*Fast Company*, April 11, 2017

WHEN YOU GET started as a college student you limit your scope. It's like, "I'm going to build this thing for the community around me." Then it's "I'm going to build this service for people on the Internet." But at some point you get to a scale where you decide we can actually solve these bigger problems that will shape the world over the next decade.

—*Vanity Fair*, September 8, 2015

If you can't think of any way that your reality can be better, then you're not thinking hard enough.

—Oculus Connect, October 12, 2017

I TRY NOT to think of things as missed opportunities as much as things that we just haven't done yet.

—Townhall Q&A in Lagos, Nigeria, August 31, 2016

YOU WATCH MOVIES about people who have different ideas, and they always portray it as there's some Eureka moment where it's like, oh, now I have this idea, and then the next thing you know we have this big company.... The reality is that that's not how the world works. And I think that's an important thing to understand, because if you think that that's how the world works, then if you personally believe that you haven't had your Eureka moment yet, then you're going to believe you can't actually go build something.

—North Carolina A&T State University,
March 13, 2017

IT'S OFTEN EASIER to predict what the world is going to be like 20 years from now than it is to predict what the world's going to be like three years from now.

—Oculus Connect, October 6, 2016

THE INTERNET IS the most powerful tool we have for creating a more open and connected world. We can't let poorly thought out laws get in the way of the Internet's development. Facebook opposes SOPA [Stop Online Piracy Act] and PIPA [Preventing Real Online Threats to Economic Creativity and Theft of Intellectual Property Act], and we will continue to oppose any laws that will hurt the Internet. The world today needs political leaders who are pro-Internet. We have been working with many of these folks for months on better alternatives to these current proposals. I encourage you to learn more about these issues and tell your congressmen that you want them to be pro-Internet.

—Facebook blog, January 18, 2012

The best way to predict the future is to create it.

—Townhall Q&A in Lagos, Nigeria, August 31, 2016

PART THREE *A Legacy in the Making*

ISN'T IT OBVIOUS that everyone was going to be on the Internet? Isn't it, like, inevitable that there would be a huge social network of people? It was something that we expected to happen. The thing that's been really surprising about the evolution of Facebook is—I think then and I think now—that if we didn't do this, someone else would have done it.

—*New Yorker*, September 20, 2010

WE DON'T THINK that a modern messaging system is going to be email. It's not email. It's a messaging system that includes email as a part of it. This is not an email killer. We don't expect anyone to say, "I'm going to shut down my Yahoo or Gmail account and switch exclusively to Facebook." We don't think that's what's happening in the world. Whether it's one day in six months, or a year, or two years, this is the way the future should work.

—*Fast Company*, October 14, 2010

THE BIGGEST RISK is not taking any risk. ... In the world that changes really quickly, the only strategy that is guaranteed to fail is not taking risks.

—Startup School, October 29, 2011

WE DON'T THINK we're anywhere near the end [of Facebook]. What we've seen is that there's this massive trend on the Internet towards there being all kinds of information available. Google came out when I was middle school. There were these search engines. Growing up, every year ... there was some new, cool thing. There were all these different services. The thing I think that's most interesting to people is other people, so I think it makes sense in a way that Facebook is by far the most engaging app that's been built online to date.

—Computer History Museum, July 21, 2010

I CERTAINLY THINK that the trend we're operating on now of helping people share information, which is really something that, going back twenty years ago, most people in society did not have the power to do; the Internet has really brought that about. Now everyone can share their opinions and information about themselves or what's going on around them, and that's a new thing. That's the trend we're hoping to push forward. That's going to be one of the most transformative trends in society over the next ten, fifteen [years], I mean, who knows how long?

—Computer History Museum, July 21, 2010

MOBILE PHONES, THE primary computing platform of today, are still organized around apps and not people.... That is not really how we process the world, it's not really how we think. And I don't think that that's how the next platform is going to work.

—Oculus Connect, October 6, 2016

WE OFTEN TALK about inventions like the printing press and the television—by simply making communication more efficient, they led to a complete transformation of many important parts of society. They gave more people a voice. They encouraged progress. They changed the way society was organized. They brought us closer together.

—*Charlie Rose*, November 7, 2011

THE MOST IMPORTANT technologies don't start off mainstream, right? In fact, a lot of them seem maybe even too crazy or complex to start. And the conventional thinkers will always say that there's going to be something more familiar that delivers enough of the value, so why build a completely new platform?

—Oculus Connect, October 12, 2017

THE THING ABOUT technology is it doesn't end, right? I mean, there's always another platform and another frontier and another way to express yourself more richly going forward.

—**Facebook Live video, September 6, 2016**

WE EXPECT GOVERNMENTS will become more responsible to issues and concerns raised directly by all their people rather than through intermediaries controlled by a select few.

—*Charlie Rose*, **November 7, 2011**

WE'RE BUILDING A web where the default is social.

—*Time*, **May 20, 2010**

I THINK THE CEO basically does two things:
They set the vision for the company, and they
recruit a team. So far, we have this vision and
we're in the middle of executing it, and we're only
four years done, so I think there's a lot left to go.
And building a team is a really important piece of
that. We spend a lot of time focused on that.

—D6 Conference, 2008

I WOULD EXPECT that next year, people will
share twice as much information as they share
this year, and the next year, they will be sharing
twice as much as they did the year before. That
means that people are using Facebook, and the
applications and the ecosystem, more and more.

—*New York Times*, November 6, 2008

AMAZON IS A great recent example of focusing on the long term and accepting shorter margins on the short term. Jeff [Bezos] went through years of people thinking he's crazy. Apple is amazing in terms of the quality of stuff that they do. And Google, too, for the same thing.

—*Wall Street Journal*, January 14, 2012

HISTORY TELLS US that systems are most fairly governed when there is an open and transparent dialogue between the people who make decisions and those who are affected by them. We believe history will one day show that this principle holds true for companies as well, and we're looking to moving in this direction with you.

—Facebook blog, February 26, 2009

I actually am always confused by companies and organizations which have the goal to try to exist forever. Like, I don't view our goal as existing forever. Our goal is to make a change in the world.

—Townhall Q&A at Facebook, September 15, 2015

I SPEND MY time thinking about how to build this and not how to exit. I think that what we're doing is more interesting than what anyone else is doing ... that this is just a cool thing to be doing. I don't spend time thinking about [an exit strategy] that much.

—**Entrepreneurial Thought Leaders Seminars, Stanford, 2005**

WE THINK THAT the future of the web will be filled with personalized experiences.... For example, now if you're logged into Facebook and go to Pandora for the first time, it can immediately start playing songs from bands you've liked across the web. And as you're playing music, it can show you friends who also like the same songs as you, and then you can click to see other music they like.

—**Facebook blog, April 21, 2010**

I'M ALSO CURIOUS about whether there is a fundamental mathematical law underlying human social relationships that governs the balance of who and what we all care about. I bet there is.

—Facebook comment, June 30, 2015

I THINK THE next five years are going to be about building out this social platform. It's about the idea that most applications are going to become social, and most industries are going to be rethought in a way where social design and doing things with your friends is at the core of how these things work.

—*Time*, December 27, 2010/January 3, 2011

As a child, many people will tell you that you don't have the skills or experience to build something that matters. I was certainly told that many times. But these days I wonder if children actually have a unique perspective to build some of the most important things. The world is changing quickly, and only a child has a full emotional understanding of what it's like to grow up today, with say, mobile phones or AI you've been able to talk to your whole conscious life.

—**Facebook post, October 7, 2017**

One reason I'm so optimistic about AI is that improvements in basic research improve systems across so many different fields—from diagnosing diseases to keep us healthy, to improving self-driving cars to keep us safe, and from showing you better content in News Feed to delivering you more relevant search results.

—**Facebook post, July 25, 2017**

THERE ARE GOING to be a few big trends. AI will continue making progress, we will be able to cure a lot more diseases in the future. We all know that. The real art is being able to see how we get from here to there.

—*Business Insider*, **February 28, 2016**

ONE OF OUR goals [for AI] for the next five to 10 years is to basically get better than human level at all of the primary human senses: vision, hearing, language, general cognition. Taste and smell, we're not that worried about. For now.

—*Fast Company*, **November 16, 2015**

JUST BECAUSE YOU can build a machine that is better than a person at something doesn't mean that it is going to have the ability to learn new domains or connect different types of information or context to do superhuman things.

—*Business Insider*, **February 28, 2016**

PEOPLE WILL ALWAYS want more immersive ways to express themselves. So if you go back ten years ago on the internet, most of what people shared and consumed was text. Now a lot of it is photos. I think, going forward, a lot of it is going to be videos, getting richer and richer.

But that is not the end. In the future, I think you are going to want to capture a whole scene, a room, to be able to transport to that.

—*Business Insider*, February 28, 2016

I DO THINK a new computing platform always emerges every 10 or 15 years. VR [Virtual Reality] is currently the most promising candidate.

—*Business Insider*, February 28, 2016

I THINK THAT the next version of the next computing platform . . . is going to be based on vision and glasses. . . . You don't have to scroll, you just look around, right? And, you know, you don't have to pull something out of your pocket, you just kind of focus a little, and it, like, pulls up what you want.

—Townhall Q&A at Facebook, September 15, 2015

[OCULUS] IS REALLY a new communication platform. By feeling truly present, you can share unbounded spaces and experiences with the people in your life. Imagine sharing not just moments with your friends online, but entire experiences and adventures.

—Facebook post, March 25, 2014

ONE OF THE most powerful side effects of VR is empathy—the ability to understand other people better when you feel like you're actually with them.

—**Facebook post, April 23, 2017**

WE ALL HAVE limits to our reality. Places we can't go, people we can't see, things we can't do. And opening up more of those experiences to all of us [with virtual reality]—that's not isolating. That's freeing.

—**Oculus Connect, October 12, 2017**

EVENTUALLY I THINK we're going to have technology where we can communicate our full sensory experience and emotions to someone through thought.

—***Vanity Fair*, September 8, 2015**

WE'RE WORKING ON a system that will let you type straight from your brain about 5x faster than you can type on your phone today. Eventually, we want to turn it into a wearable technology that can be manufactured at scale. Even a simple yes/no "brain click" would help make things like augmented reality feel much more natural.

Technology is going to have to get a lot more advanced before we can share a pure thought or feeling, but this is a first step.

—Facebook post, April 19, 2017

Philanthropy

A LOT OF people wait until later in their careers to think about how to give back, and I just had a bunch of conversations with my friends and people who I work with recently where it really occurred to me, "Why wait another 15 or 20 years when I'll have a lot more time to focus on it, but if we already have the resources we should probably get started on it now." Hopefully, participating in this encourages other people in our generation to do so as well.

—*Time*, 2010

WE BELIEVE ALL lives have equal value, and that includes the many more people who will live in future generations than live today. Our society has an obligation to invest now to improve the lives of all those coming into this world, not just those already here.

—**letter written to daughter Max Zuckerberg, December 1, 2015**

Our hopes for your generation focus on two ideas: advancing human potential and promoting equality.

Advancing human potential is about pushing the boundaries on how great a human life can be.... Promoting equality is about making sure everyone has access to these opportunities—regardless of the nation, families or circumstances they are born into.

—letter written to daughter Max Zuckerberg,
December 1, 2015

Bill Gates offered me some advice: Don't just give your money away—it's something that requires practice to get good at. So why wait? Clearly I have a day job that takes up 99 percent of my time, so I can't be running a foundation. But I can take a venture capital approach, where you invest in people.

—*Wired,* April 4, 2013

As you begin the next generation of the Chan Zuckerberg family, we also begin the Chan Zuckerberg Initiative to join people across the world to advance human potential and promote equality for all children in the next generation. Our initial areas of focus will be personalized learning, curing disease, connecting people and building strong communities.

We will give 99% of our Facebook shares—currently about $45 billion—during our lives to advance this mission.

—letter written to daughter Max Zuckerberg,
December 1, 2015

OUR APPROACH AT the Chan Zuckerberg Initiative is to bring engineering to social change. We build tools to bring personalized learning into more schools and help scientists cure all diseases in our children's lifetime. Part of creating sustainable social change is also helping to build movements around these issues—to fight for more science funding and better education for all children.

—Facebook post, January 10, 2017

WE LOOK FOR opportunities to bring engineering to social change, because there are lots of people who can invest capital and hard work, but when you can also build tools, when you can empower people to go out in the world and make change for themselves, that's when the biggest change happens.

—Chan Zuckerberg Initiative announcement,
September 21, 2016

THE POINT OF philanthropy is to try new ideas and be the research-and-development [arm] for the public. We want to make sure that [personalized learning], which seems like a good hypothesis and approach, gets a good shot at getting tested and implemented.

—*Education Week*, March 7, 2016

THERE ARE MANY different challenges all facing education at once. Teaching needs to be more respected and revered as a career. School districts need more autonomy and clearer leadership so they can be managed more like startups than like government bureaucracies. And outside the classroom, we need to support students' interests, give them a safe environment to grow up in, and keep everyone healthy.

—on a $100 million donation to a foundation to benefit Newark, New Jersey, schools, Startup: Education, Facebook, September 24, 2010

IN THE U.S., we invest about 50 times more in treating people who are sick than in finding cures so people don't get sick in the first place. You only would do that if you believed that people were always going to get sick.

—**APEC CEO Summit, November 19, 2016**

A FEW YEARS ago I taught a class on entrepreneurship at a local middle school. Some of my best students were undocumented. Because of that, they weren't sure if they would be able to go to college. These are smart and hardworking kids who could grow up to be leaders in their communities and in the world. But despite having lived in the US for as long as they can remember, they could be denied the chance to participate fully in the life of our country and reach their potential.

—**Facebook post, March 8, 2016**

THE DECISION TO end DACA [Deferred Action for Childhood Arrivals] is not just wrong. It is particularly cruel to offer young people the American Dream, encourage them to come out of the shadows and trust our government, and then punish them for it.

—Facebook post, September 5, 2017

IN THIS CENTURY, global development and global connectivity are closely linked. If you want to help people feed, heal, educate and employ themselves around the world, we need to connect the world as well.

—written with Bono, *New York Times*, September 26, 2015

FACEBOOK IS REALLY about communicating
and telling stories. . . . We think that people can
really help spread awareness of organ donation
and that they want to participate in this to their
friends. And that can be a big part of helping
solve the crisis that's out there. . . . We want
to make it simple. You just put in the state or
country that you're from, so that we can help link
you to the official registries.

—*ABC News*, May 1, 2012

FACEBOOK IS ABOUT connecting and sharing—
connecting with your friends, family and
communities, and sharing information with them
about your life, work, school, and interests. . . .
What has amazed us over the past eight years
is how people use these same tools and social
dynamics to address important issues and
challenges in their communities. Last year in
Missouri, Facebook users tracked down and
returned treasured mementos to families who
thought they'd lost everything in the Joplin
tornado. In Japan, people used Facebook to
locate family and friends following the 2011
earthquake and tsunami. Smaller acts of
kindness happen millions of times a day on
Facebook. . . . Even one individual can have an
outsized impact on the challenges facing another,
and on the world. At Facebook, we call that the
power of friends.

—*ABC News*, May 2, 2012

THE INTERNET IS so important that for every 10 people who gain internet access, about one person is lifted out of poverty and about one new job is created.

—letter written to daughter Max Zuckerberg,
December 1, 2015

WE USE THINGS like Facebook to share news and keep in touch with our friends, but in those [developing] countries, they'll use this for deciding what kind of government they want to have. Getting access to health care information for the first time ever. Staying connected to someone a hundred miles away in a different village that they haven't seen in a decade.

—*Wired*, August 26, 2013

WE ASKED A bunch of folks who were involved
in containing the [ebola] outbreak, "What can
we do to help?" and the No. 1 thing that they said
was "Help us get connectivity because we need
to be able to wire up all these different Ebola
treatment units to make it so we can coordinate
the response, so people know and can count the
people who have come into contact with the
people who have Ebola."

—*Studio 1.0*, February 19, 2015

TODAY WE CAN only hear the voices and witness
the imaginations of one-third of the world's
people. We are all being robbed of the creativity
and potential of the two-thirds of the world not
yet online. Tomorrow, if we succeed, the Internet
will truly represent everyone.

—*Wall Street Journal*, July 7, 2014

What we figured out was that in order to get everyone in the world to have basic access to the Internet, that's a problem that's probably billions of dollars. Or maybe low tens of billions. With the right innovation, that's actually within the range of affordability.

—*Time*, December 15, 2014

THERE'S NO WAY we can draw a plan about why we're going to invest billions of dollars in getting mostly poor people online. But at some level, we believe this is what we're here to do, and we think it's going to be good, and if we do it, some of that value will come back to us.

—*Wired*, January 19, 2016

TODAY, THERE ARE three main barriers that are preventing people from connecting—and we can fix them all. First is availability. The idea is, you might have a phone, but there's no network around you to connect to. . . . The second is affordability. . . . There may be a network around you, but you can't afford either to buy a phone or to connect to the network. . . . And the third barrier is awareness. And this is actually, interestingly enough, the biggest barrier that has the most people in it, is people who have a phone and there is a network around them that they can connect to and they can afford to connect to it . . . but they're not sure why they would want to.

—APEC CEO Summit, November 19, 2016

CONNECTING EVERYONE IS going to be something that no single company can do by themselves.... Internet.org is a partnership between a number of different technology companies and nonprofits and governments.

—*Studio 1.0*, February 19, 2015

IF WHAT I cared about was making more money, I would take the engineers and the people who are working on Internet.org and spreading connectivity around the world and have them go work on our ads products.

—Townhall Q&A in Bogotá, Colombia,
January 14, 2015

THE INFRASTRUCTURE TO build what supports
the internet, all the pipes and the fiber, people
invest hundreds of billions of dollars a year
across the world in building that. So, at some
point, someone needs to pay to make that. . . .
It can't just be built for free. But what we can
do is make it so that everyone in the world can
get some basic services for free, and that's what
Internet.org is doing.

—Townhall Q&A in Bogotá, Colombia,
January 14, 2015

I'M NEVER GOING to say that internet is more
important than food or clean water. I really think
people need both to be in a modern society, but I
really think that we're much better suited to help
out in providing the internet to people than clean
water. That's just not the company that we are.

—Q&A with the media in India, October 9, 2014

I THINK THAT there needs to be a 911 for the internet, where even if you haven't bought a data plan or can afford that, you can get free access to some basic services for health, education, jobs, communication.

—Internet.org Summit, October 9, 2014

WE LAUNCHED FREE Basics, a set of basic internet services for things like education, healthcare, jobs and communication that people can use without paying for data.... Free Basics is a bridge to the full internet and digital equality.

—*Times of India*, December 28, 2015

I THINK THE future is going to be thousands of solar-powered planes on the outskirts of places where people live. That's going to make connectivity both much more available and cheaper.

—*The Verge*, July 21, 2016

IN SOME COMMUNITIES, people can't connect because it's just not culturally acceptable. Our research has found that, in developing countries, 25 percent fewer women than men are connected to the internet. And, you know, if we want to live up to our full potential, we really need an internet where every woman has the right to get connected and get online.

—Internet.org Summit, October 9, 2014

MILESTONES

1984

- Mark Zuckerberg is born in White Plains, New York, on May 14 to Karen and Edward Zuckerberg. (The family later moves to Dobbs Ferry, New York, where he and his sisters were raised. His parents still live there.)

1996

- Zuckerberg creates Zucknet, a messaging program written in Atari BASIC. It is used by his father, a dentist, at work and also at home.

1998

- SEPTEMBER: Zuckerberg enrolls in Ardsley High School, where he excelled in the classics.

2000

- SEPTEMBER: Zuckerberg enrolls in Phillips Exeter Academy, a prestigious prep school.

2001

- Under the company name of Intelligent Media Group, Zuckerberg builds a media player called Synapse. Both AOL and Microsoft try to buy the program, but Zuckerberg declines.

2002

- JUNE: Zuckerberg graduates from Phillips Exeter Academy, where he won prizes in science and classical studies and captained the fencing team.

- SEPTEMBER: Zuckerberg begins first year at Harvard University, where he joins a Jewish fraternity, Alpha Epsilon Pi.

2003

- Zuckerberg writes CourseMatch, software designed to link Harvard students with the courses they are taking; he also writes Facemash, which juxtaposes photos of female students for users to evaluate who is "hotter."

- Zuckerberg meets his future wife, Priscilla Chan, at a frat party at Alpha Epsilon Pi.

2004

- FEBRUARY 4: Working out of his dormitory room at Harvard with Dustin Moskovitz, Eduardo Saverin, and Chris Hughes, Zuckerberg posts the first iteration of Facebook on the Internet: Thefacebook.com. It is available exclusively to the Harvard community.

- MARCH: Zuckerberg expands reach of his fledgling website to a select few other schools, including Stanford, Columbia, and Yale.

- JUNE: Zuckerberg drops out of Harvard to further develop his social networking site. He moves to Palo Alto, California, where he and his friends rent a suburban ranch home that doubles as an office.

- AUGUST: Zuckerberg launches Wirehog, a peer-to-peer file-sharing service.

- SEPTEMBER: Zuckerberg launches the Facebook Wall.

- SEPTEMBER: A lawsuit filed by Cameron and Tyler Winklevoss and Divya Narendra claims Zuckerberg ripped off the key ideas of the social networking site they were developing (HarvardConnection.com).

- Thefacebook hits 1 million users.

2005

- MAY 6: Accel Partners invest $13 million in Zuckerberg's company.

- MAY TO OCTOBER: Zuckerberg expands the reach of the social network to US colleges, high schools, and international schools.

- AUGUST: Zuckerberg changes the company name to Facebook, after buying the domain name facebook. com for a reported $200,000. (Sean Parker suggested to Mark that he simplify the company name from Thefacebook to Facebook.)

- OCTOBER: Facebook launches a photo sharing service.

- Facebook hits 6 million users.

2006

- MAY: Facebook opens up to business networks. Yahoo's offer to buy Facebook for $1 billion is declined.

- SEPTEMBER: Facebook opens up to anyone 13 years old or older.

- DECEMBER: Facebook hits 12 million users.

2007

- MARCH: The lawsuit filed by the Winklevosses and Narendra is dismissed without prejudice, but is subsequently refiled.

- MAY 24: Facebook launches Facebook Platform, for programmers wishing to write social applications.

- AUGUST: MIT Technology Review cites Zuckerberg as one of the top 35 innovators under 35.

- OCTOBER: Microsoft's CEO Steve Ballmer offers to buy Facebook for $15 billion. Zuckerberg says no. Instead, Microsoft buys a $240 million stake in the company.

- Facebook hits 58 million users.

2008

- JANUARY: Zuckerberg wins *Techcrunch*'s Crunchie Award for Best Startup CEO.

- JUNE: The Winklevoss/Narendra lawsuit is settled out of court.

- Facebook hits 145 million users.

2009

- JANUARY: Zuckerberg starts his annual personal challenges with a resolution to wear a tie every day.

- FEBRUARY: Facebook introduces the Like button for use on its own website as well as third-party websites.

- DECEMBER: Facebook hits 360 million users.

2010

- JANUARY: Zuckerberg's personal challenge is to learn Mandarin.

- JULY 21: Facebook hits 500 million users.

- SEPTEMBER: Zuckerberg donates $100 million to the Newark, New Jersey, public school system. Priscilla Chan, a medical student, moves into Zuckerberg's Palo Alto house, which he rents.

- SEPTEMBER: *New Statesman* magazine ranks him as number 16 of the world's 50 most influential figures.

- OCTOBER 1: *The Social Network*, a motion picture directed by David Fincher and based on Ben Mezrich's nonfiction book *The Accidental Billionaires*, is released.

- OCTOBER 3: In an episode of *The Simpsons* titled "Loan-a-Lisa," Zuckerberg lends his voice to his own cartoon character.

- OCTOBER: *Vanity Fair* ranks Zuckerberg as number 1 of the 100 "most influential people of the Information Age."

- DECEMBER: *Time* magazine names Zuckerberg Person of the Year.

- DECEMBER: Zuckerberg promises to give away half his fortune to charity, joining Microsoft cofounder Bill Gates and investor Warren Buffett in the Giving Pledge.

- Facebook hits 608 million users.

2011

- JANUARY: Zuckerberg's personal challenge is to eat only animals that he has killed himself throughout the year.

- Facebook introduces a new feature, Timeline.

- JANUARY 29: Zuckerberg appears as a surprise guest on *Saturday Night Live*, as does Jesse Eisenberg, who portrayed him in *The Social Network*.

- MARCH: Facebook hosts its first worldwide programming competition, the Facebook Hacker Cup.

- APRIL 10: Zuckerberg announces on his Timeline that Facebook has acquired Instagram.

- Zuckerberg buys a house for $7 million in Palo Alto, California.

- DECEMBER: Facebook moves to its new corporate offices at 1601 Willow Road, Menlo Park, California. (1 Hacker Way is the address for a ring road around its East Campus.)

2012

- JANUARY: Zuckerberg's personal challenge for the year is to write code every day.

- MAY 18: Facebook's initial public offering sells at $38 a share, raising $16 billion for a market cap of $104 billion.

- MAY 19: Zuckerberg marries Priscilla Chan, which he announces by posting a "life event" on his Facebook page. (Guests, who numbered fewer than 100, had no inkling they were invited to a wedding. They thought it was a celebratory party for Chan's graduation from medical school.)

- JUNE: Facebook hits 955 million users.

- OCTOBER: Zuckerberg announces that Facebook hit the 1 billion mark. He remarks, "Well, just everyone came together and counted down. Then we all went back to work."

2013

- JANUARY: Zuckerberg's 2013 personal challenge is to meet someone new every day who doesn't work at Facebook.

- FEBRUARY 13: Zuckerberg holds a fundraiser at his home for governor of New Jersey Chris Christie. Zuckerberg had previously worked with Christie on education reform in New Jersey's public schools. The Facebook CEO faces some backlash for his support of a conservative politician.

- FEBRUARY 20: Alongside Chan, Sergey Brin, Anne Wojcicki, Art Levinson, and Yuri Milner, Zuckerberg announces the creation of the Breakthrough Prize in Life Sciences, which awards pioneering scientists, engineers, and researchers with individual prizes of $3 million each year.

- APRIL 4: Zuckerberg reveals that, at Chan's urging, he has been teaching an after-school class on entrepreneurship to middle school students.

- APRIL 4: Zuckerberg announces Facebook Home, a download for Android phones that puts its family of apps on the home screen. He also unveils the First phone, to be launched with HTC.

- APRIL 10: Zuckerberg announces the creation of FWD.us, an organization made up of leaders in the tech community who want to advocate for bipartisan immigration reform in the United States.

- JUNE: Leaked documents reveal that the NSA has access to the servers of Facebook, Google, and Apple through a program called Prism. Zuckerberg denies that Facebook has ever allowed the federal government access to its servers.

- AUGUST 21: Facebook launches Internet.org, a partnership with tech companies, local governments, and mobile operators, in order to provide internet access in remote locations.

2014

- JANUARY: Zuckerberg announces that his personal challenge for the year is to write at least one thank-you note each day.

- FEBRUARY 19: Facebook announces plans to acquire WhatsApp, a mobile messaging company, for about $19 billion.

- MARCH 13: Zuckerberg calls President Barack Obama to express his frustration over a report (based on documents leaked by Edward Snowden) that reveals the nature and extent of the NSA's internet surveillance programs.

- MARCH 21: Along with other tech executives, Zuckerberg attends a meeting with President Obama at the White House to discuss technology, privacy, and security.

- MARCH 25: Facebook agrees to acquire Oculus VR, which manufactures virtual reality technology.

- MARCH 27: Facebook starts its Connectivity Lab, a team dedicated to researching and building communication and aerospace technology to enable global internet connectivity.

- MAY 27: A judge in Iran summons Zuckerberg to court to answer charges that Instagram and WhatsApp violate users' privacy. Zuckerberg doesn't answer the summons.

- JUNE 24: A paper in the *Proceedings of the National Academy of Sciences* reveals that Facebook had manipulated users' News Feeds to test the emotional responses users had to certain posts and articles.

- OCTOBER 15: Facebook introduces Safety Check, a feature that allows users to mark themselves safe if they are in an area where a crisis or disaster recently occurred.

- NOVEMBER 18: Facebook launches its Groups app.

2015

- JANUARY: Zuckerberg announces that his personal challenge for 2015 is to read a new book every other week.

- FEBRUARY 6: Zuckerberg and Chan announce a $75 million donation to San Francisco General Hospital, where Chan served as a medical resident.

- MARCH: Facebook's employees move into the new building in Menlo Park. The building, known as MPK 20, was designed by Frank Gehry and was touted as having the largest open-floor plan (40,000 square feet) in the world.

- JUNE 11: Oculus introduces the Rift, a consumer-facing virtual-reality headset.

- JULY 30: Facebook completes construction of Aquila, a solar-powered plane intended to beam internet around the world.

- OCTOBER 5: Facebook announces plans to partner with Eutelsat to launch a satellite into space that would enable internet connectivity in parts of Africa.

- NOVEMBER 20: Oculus begins shipping the first virtual reality product for consumers, the Samsung Gear VR.

- NOVEMBER 30: Zuckerberg and Chan's daughter Max is born. The family accompanies the birth announcement with the introduction of the Chan Zuckerberg Initative, a philanthropic effort funded by 99 percent of the couple's Facebook shares. The initiative's broad goal is to make the world a better place for Max's generation. Some of the initiative's efforts include education, medical research, and criminal justice reform.

- DECEMBER: A judge in Brazil bans WhatsApp after the company refuses to hand over messages sent through the app, which uses end-to-end encrypted data making messages impossible to access. This is the first of four times (as of this writing) that the app would be banned by courts in Brazil.

2016

- JANUARY: Zuckerberg announces a dual personal challenge for 2016: to run 365 miles and to build a simple AI system for his own home.

- FEBRUARY 8: India's Telecom Regulatory Authority establishes net neutrality rules that ban Facebook's Free Basics program, which favored some internet providers over others based on the services they provided, effectively reducing the competitive power of smaller providers.

- FEBRUARY 24: Facebook launches five additional Reactions to supplement the long-standing Like button.

- APRIL 5: Facebook begins rolling out automatic alt text, a service that uses speech to identify posts and photographs on the Facebook screen for blind users.

- APRIL 6: Facebook launches its Live video feature, which allows users to record video to Facebook in real time.

- APRIL 13: Zuckerberg commits to join an initiative with Stephen Hawking and Yuri Milner that will invest in small spacecraft to explore stars beyond our nearby planets.

- APRIL 27: Zuckerberg announces a proposal to reclassify Facebook's stocks. The proposal would essentially allow Zuckerberg to retain voting control at Facebook while also selling 99 percent of his shares to fund the Chan Zuckerberg Initiative. A few days later, a Facebook shareholder files a proposed class action lawsuit to halt the reclassification.

- MAY: A leaked document reveals that Facebook uses editorial oversight, in addition to AI, when choosing its Trending Topics. Documentation previously supplied to users did not reveal the extent of the editorial oversight. Several conservative outlets accuse Facebook of having a liberal bias, which Zuckerberg counters by inviting prominent conservatives to have a public conversation with him.

- JULY 6: The shooting of Philando Castile, a black man, by a police officer in Minnesota is captured on Facebook Live by his girlfriend, Diamond Reynolds.

- JULY 6: Facebook introduces OpenCellular, an open-source wireless access platform intended to enable internet connectivity in remote parts of the world.

- JUNE 28: Aquila completes its first successful flight.

- SEPTEMBER 1: The SpaceX Falcon 9 rocket contracted to carry Facebook's satellite into space explodes two days before its scheduled launch, destroying the satellite that was meant to enable internet connectivity in areas of Africa.

- OCTOBER 3: Facebook launches its Marketplace tab, allowing users to buy and sell products through a dedicated platform on the site.

- NOVEMBER: News outlets report that Facebook is developing a censorship tool to get access to China.

- NOVEMBER: News outlets, politicians, and even Obama claim that partisan fake news—planted by both conservative and liberal sources—spread on Facebook had an influence on the outcome of the presidential election. At the Techonomy conference Zuckerberg argues that, if anything, Facebook had a positive influence on the electorate, getting people informed and to the polls.

- DECEMBER 15: Facebook and Zuckerberg appear to change positions on the influence of fake news, announcing that the site will make an effort to remove and reduce its spread on Facebook.

2017

- JANUARY 3: Zuckerberg announces that his 2017 personal challenge is to visit every state where he hasn't been before.

- JANUARY 4: A Facebook Live video shows four Chicago teenagers torturing a mentally disabled young man. The video is removed from the website, but its release reignites conversations about the new frontiers of online streaming and Facebook's responsibility to monitor user content.

- JANUARY 11: Facebook introduces the Facebook Journalism Project, a collaboration with news services that promotes high-quality journalism and creates products to help reporters do their work.

- JANUARY 17: Zuckerberg testifies in court about the deal to acquire Oculus after the virtual-reality company was accused of stealing technology. Zuckerberg denies that Oculus ever stole technology.

- APRIL 16: A video of the murder of Robert Godwin Sr. by Steve Stephens is posted on Facebook and is not removed for several hours. The video raises controversy around Facebook's community standards.

- MAY 3: Facebook adds 3,000 people to its community operations team in an attempt to address violence and hate speech in Facebook videos and News Feeds.

- JUNE 22: Zuckerberg announces Facebook's new mission statement: enable users bring the world closer together and build global community.

- JUNE 27: Facebook grows to 2 billion members.

- MAY 25: Zuckerberg delivers the commencement address at Harvard University.

- JULY 7: Facebook announces its plans for Willow Campus, a "mixed-use village" in Menlo Park that would provide reduce-price and full-price housing as well as office space, retail space, and community centers. The first occupants would be able to move in in 2021.

- AUGUST: Zuckerberg and Chan's second daughter, August, is born.

- AUGUST 28: Facebook announces that it will no longer allow Pages that repeatedly share false news stories to purchase ads on the platform.

- SEPTEMBER 21: Zuckerberg announces his intention to crack down on fake news from untrustworthy and biased sources, particularly foreign actors interfering in politics and elections around the world.

- SEPTEMBER: The *New York Times* and other outlets report that Facebook has handed over to Congress over 3,000 ads that had been planted on the website by Russian actors in order to influence the 2016 election, apparently in favor of Trump.

- SEPTEMBER 22: Zuckerberg retracts his proposal to reclassify Facebook stock. He writes that, with the social media network's success, he can both retain voting control at Facebook and fund the Chan Zuckerberg Initiative without reclassifying stock.

- SEPTEMBER 27: President Donald Trump tweets that Facebook was "always anti-Trump." Zuckerberg responds on Facebook, arguing that the social media network is a platform for all ideas and people.

- OCTOBER 11: Oculus introduces the Oculus Go, a virtual-reality headset that doesn't require cables or any other attachments.

- OCTOBER 27: In an effort to make campaign donations more transparent, Zuckerberg announces new standards for reporting the funding sources of political ads on Facebook.

- OCTOBER 31: Representatives from Facebook testify before Congress on the influence Russia had on the election. Facebook believed that 120 pages created by Russian actors had created 80,000 posts spread to 29 million US users.

- NOVEMBER 27: Facebook launches AI tools that can evaluate suicidal postings in Facebook and alert administrators of its possibility.

2018

- JANUARY 4: Zuckerberg announces that his personal challenge for 2018 is to fix Facebook's system in order to prevent misuse like the kind that occurred before the 2016 presidential election.

- MARCH: News outlets reveal that Cambridge Analytica, a firm hired to help in Donald Trump's presidential campaign, was able to access private information from 50 million users without their permission.